S0-ECN-723

Family Circle | casserole cookbook

Family Circle®

CASSEROLE COOKBOOK

A Practical Guide to creative cooking containing special material from Family Circle Magazine and the Family Circle Illustrated Library of Cooking

ROCKVILLE HOUSE PUBLISHERS
GARDEN CITY, NEW YORK 11530

on the cover:
The French taught the world how to cook in a casserole, and **Beef Burgundy** is a classic example of this type of cooking.

on the back cover:
Dazzle company with **Busy-Day Lamb Ragout** (bottom) or make **Quiche Lorraine,** using convenience foods for a quick main-dish.

opposite the title page:
Use a Dutch oven, a black bean pot, a casserole dish, or a crockery pot, and **Glazed Cornish Hens** and **Vermont Corned Beef Platter** are winners.

Publishing Staff

Editor: MALCOLM E. ROBINSON
Design and Layout: MARGOT L. WOLF
Production Editor: DONALD D. WOLF

For Family Circle

Editorial Director: ARTHUR M. HETTICH
Editor Family Circle Books: MARIE T. WALSH
Assistant Editor: CERI E. HADDA

Printed in the United States of America

A QUICK METRIC TABLE FOR COOKS

Liquid Measures

Metric	Equivalent	U.S.	Metric
1 liter	4¼ cups (1 quart + ¼ cup *or* 34 fluid ounces)	1 gallon	3.785 liters
1 demiliter (½ liter)	2⅛ cups (1 pint + ⅛ cups *or* 17 fluid ounces)	1 quart	0.946 liter
1 deciliter (1/10 liter)	A scant ½ cup *or* 3.4 fluid ounces	1 pint	0.473 liter
1 centiliter (1/100 liter)	Approximately 2 teaspoons *or* .34 fluid ounce	1 cup	0.237 liter *or* 237 milliliters
1 milliliter (1/1000 liter)	Approximately 1/5 teaspoon *or* .034 fluid ounce	1 tbsp.	Approximately 1.5 centiliters *or* 15 milliliters

Weights

Metric	Equivalent	U.S.	Metric
1 kilogram	2.205 pounds	1 pound	0.454 kilogram *or* 453.6 grams
500 grams	1.103 pounds *or* about 17.5 ounces	½ pound	0.226 kilogram *or* 226.8 grams
100 grams	3.5 ounces	¼ pound	0.113 kilogram *or* 113.4 grams
10 grams	.35 ounce	1 ounce	28.35 grams
1 gram	0.035 ounce		

Linear Measures

Metric	Equivalent	U.S.	Metric
1 meter	1.09 yards *or* 3.28 feet *or* 39.37 inches	1 yard	0.914 meter
1 decimeter (1/10 meter)	3.93 inches	1 foot	0.3048 meter *or* 3.048 decimeters *or* 30.48 centimeters
1 centimeter (1/100 meter)	0.39 inch	1 inch	2.54 centimeters *or* 25.4 millimeters
1 millimeter (1/1000 meter)	0.039 inch		

Contents

Take red cabbage and apples and some Polish sausage, simmer in a casserole, and the result is a delectable **Polish Hot Pot** (in the Crock Pot section).

Introduction

WHEN YOU ARE looking for a meal that will suit your family or for company, leave it to a casserole. Easy to prepare, time saving, and nutritionally well-balanced, casseroles suit any occasion.

Stemming from the French words, "en casse," a casserole means a meal in a dish or the dish itself. So you have a complete meal which is served in one dish.

Although you can do so if you want, there is no need to add any side dishes. You pop all the ingredients into one pot—a Dutch oven, casserole dish, baking dish, or the most recent up-date version of the old Dutch oven, an electric slow cooker—sit back and wait for the meal to cook itself.

This makes a casserole especially good for company fare. While the meal cooks, you can settle back and spend time with your guests instead of fussing in the kitchen. And if you put up the meal and shred the vegetables the night before, this complete make-ahead cooked in one meal dish allows you time to prepare for your guests so that you are relaxed before the doorbell rings.

And best of all, in this day and age when we all are on the go so much that a snack at noon-day is often all we can get, a one-pot meal can be nutritionally well-balanced.

So enjoy your **Casserole Cookbook.** It has been designed with easy reference in mind.

One-Dish Meals

Have you ever wanted to create a casserole, had the meat in mind, but not known what to do? This chapter has casseroles arranged in meat order—beef first, then veal, lamb, ham and pork, poultry, and finally vegetables—so that you can select a casserole that suits your needs at a flip of a page.

BEEF

Beef and Kidney Pie

Meat and vegetables bake lazily in a pastry jacket. Pastry calls for bacon drippings to cut the cost, yet add extra flavor

Bake at 400° for 1 hour and 10 minutes.
Makes 6 servings

6 lamb kidneys (about 12 ounces)
1 pound lean boneless beef chuck
Instant unseasoned meat tenderizer
Savory Pastry (recipe follows)
4 medium-size potatoes, pared and sliced thin (3 cups)
1 large onion, peeled and sliced
3 tablespoons flour
1 teaspoon salt
½ teaspoon leaf thyme, crumbled
Dash of ground allspice
¾ cup water
1 teaspoon Worcestershire sauce

1 Soak kidneys overnight in lightly salted water to cover; drain. Halve lengthwise; cut out tubes and white membrane. (Scissors do a neat quick job.) Dice meat.
2 Trim any excess fat from beef; moisten meat and sprinkle with tenderizer, following label directions; cut meat into ½-inch cubes.
3 Try out enough fat trimmings to make 2 tablespoons drippings in a medium-size frying pan; discard trimmings.
4 Brown beef cubes in drippings in frying pan; remove with a slotted spoon and set aside. Sauté kidneys in drippings in same pan, stirring often, just until meat loses its pink color; remove and combine with beef.
5 Prepare *Savory Pastry*. Roll out two thirds to a 12-inch round on a lightly floured pastry cloth or board; fit into a deep 9-inch pie plate; trim overhang to ½ inch.
6 Combine potatoes and onion in a medium-size bowl; sprinkle with flour, salt, thyme, and allspice; toss to coat well. Layer half of the vegetable mixture, all of the meat, and remaining vegetable mixture into prepared pastry shell. Mix water and Worcestershire sauce in a cup; drizzle over filling.
7 Roll out remaining pastry to an 11-inch round; cut several slits near center to let steam escape; cover pie. Trim overhang to 1 inch; turn edges under, flush with rim; flute.
8 Bake in hot oven (400°) 1 hour and 10 minutes, or until meat and vegetables are tender and pastry is richly golden. Let stand 15 minutes, then cut into wedges.

SAVORY PASTRY—Measure 2 cups sifted all-purpose flour into a medium-size bowl; cut in ½ cup chilled bacon drippings with a pastry blender until mixture is crumbly. Sprinkle with 5 tablespoons water, 1 tablespoon at a time; mix lightly with a fork just until pastry holds together and leaves side of bowl clean. (If you do not have bacon drippings, use ⅔ cup vegetable shortening plus ½ teaspoon salt.)

Jiffy Cassoulet

An easy-to-do version of the French classic mixture of beans and meat

Bake at 350° for 1 hour.
Makes 8 servings

6 slices bacon
2 pounds meat-loaf mixture (ground beef and pork)
1 can (about 1 pound) red kidney beans, drained
1 can (about 1 pound) white kidney beans, drained
1 can (about 1 pound) sliced carrots, drained
1 can (about 1 pound) stewed tomatoes
1 tablespoon dried parsley flakes
2 teaspoons salt
1 teaspoon leaf thyme, crumbled
¼ teaspoon pepper

1 Sauté bacon just until fat starts to cook out

(continued)

in a large frying pan; remove and drain on paper toweling; set aside.
2 Shape meat-loaf mixture into a large patty in same pan; brown 5 minutes on each side. Pour off all drippings, then break meat up into chunks.
3 Stir in drained beans and carrots, tomatoes, and seasonings; heat to boiling. Spoon into a greased 10-cup baking dish; place bacon on top.
4 Bake in moderate oven (350°) 1 hour, or until bubbly hot and bacon is crisp.

Scandinavian Ragout

Dill and sour cream flavor this casserole combining meat, potatoes, cucumber and corn

Bake at 350° about 30 minutes.
Makes 6 servings

1 pound ground beef
½ pound ground veal
1 cup soft bread crumbs (about 2 slices)
1 egg
1 small can evaporated milk (⅔ cup)
1 tablespoon grated onion
1 teaspoon grated lemon peel
1 teaspoon salt (for meat balls)
4 tablespoons vegetable shortening
6 medium-size (about 2 pounds) potatoes, pared and cut as for French-frying
1 medium-size cucumber, halved lengthwise and sliced ¼ inch thick
1 can (12 or 16 ounces) whole-kernel corn
1 tablespoon all-purpose flour
½ teaspoon salt (for gravy)
⅛ teaspoon pepper
1 cup (8-ounce carton) dairy sour cream
1 tablespoon dill weed

1 Mix beef, veal, bread crumbs, egg, evaporated milk, onion, lemon peel, and 1 teaspoon salt in large bowl; shape into 36 small balls. Brown on all sides in shortening in medium-size frying pan; place in mound in one third of buttered 12-cup baking dish.
2 Boil potato strips in salted water 5 minutes; transfer with slotted spoon to baking dish, piling in mound to fill second third of dish; save potato water for Step 4.
3 Boil cucumber slices in salted water 3 minutes; drain, adding liquid to potato water. Drain corn, adding liquid to potato-cucumber water, if needed, to make 1 cup. Toss corn with cucumbers; spoon into remaining space in baking dish.
4 Blend flour, ½ teaspoon salt, and pepper into fat in frying pan; slowly stir in the 1 cup of saved vegetable liquid. Cook, stirring constantly, until gravy thickens and boils 1 minute. Stir in sour cream and dill weed; heat just to boiling; pour over potatoes and meat; tip dish so gravy will flow evenly to bottom; cover.
5 Bake in moderate oven (350°) 30 minutes, or until bubbly-hot.

Beef Crepes Continental

The popular crepe in a different style—filled with a ground beef mixture and baked in a cheese sauce

Bake at 375° for 20 minutes.
Makes 6 servings

Basic Crêpes (recipe follows)
5 tablespoons butter or margarine
3 tablespoons flour
1 teaspoon salt
¼ teaspoon pepper
2 cups milk
½ cup light cream or table cream
1 cup grated Parmesan cheese
1 medium-size onion, chopped (½ cup)
1½ pounds ground beef
1 can (3 or 4 ounces) chopped mushrooms

1 Make *Basic Crêpes* and bake; set aside while making sauce and filling.
2 Melt 4 tablespoons of the butter or margarine in a medium-size saucepan; blend in flour, ½ teaspoon of the salt, and ⅛ teaspoon of the pepper. Cook, stirring constantly, until bubbly. Stir in milk and cream; continue cooking and stirring until sauce thickens and boils 1 minute; remove from heat. Stir in ¾ cup of the Parmesan cheese; keep warm.
3 Sauté onion in remaining 1 tablespoon butter or margarine until soft in a large frying pan; push to one side.
4 Shape ground beef into a large patty; place in same pan. Brown 5 minutes on each side, then break up into chunks. Stir in ½ cup of the cheese sauce, mushrooms and liquid, and remaining ½ teaspoon salt and ⅛ teaspoon pepper.
5 Spoon 2 tablespoonfuls of the meat filling onto each baked crêpe; roll up tightly, jelly-roll fashion. Place in a baking pan, 13x9x2; spoon remaining cheese sauce over top. Sprinkle with the remaining ¼ cup Parmesan cheese.
6 Bake in moderate oven (375°) 20 minutes, or until bubbly.

Basic Crêpes—Sift ¾ cup all-purpose flour and ½ teaspoon salt into a medium-size bowl. Beat 3 eggs with 1 cup milk and 1 tablespoon vegetable oil until blended in a small bowl; beat into flour mixture until smooth. Measure batter, a scant ¼ cup at a time, into a heated well-buttered 7-inch frying pan, tilting pan to cover bottom completely. Bake 1 to 2 minutes, or until tops are set and undersides are golden; turn. Bake 1 to 2 minutes longer, or until bottoms brown. Repeat with remaining batter to make 12 crêpes, buttering pan before each baking.

Beef and Onion Supreme

Ground beef and Bermuda onions baked in cream are sure to become a family favorite

Bake at 375° for 1 hour.
Makes 6 servings

3 medium-size Bermuda onions
1½ pounds ground chuck
1 large clove of garlic, crushed
1 package (10 ounces) frozen chopped spinach
1 teaspoon salt
1 teaspoon leaf rosemary, crumbled
¼ teaspoon pepper
1 envelope instant chicken broth or 1 teaspoon granulated chicken bouillon
1¼ cups water
1 cup light cream or table cream
1 cup soft white bread crumbs (2 slices)
2 tablespoons butter or margarine, melted

1 Cook unpeeled onions in boiling salted water 15 minutes; drain. Let stand until cool enough to handle, then peel and cut in half.
2 While onions cook, brown ground chuck in a large skillet; remove with a slotted spoon; reserve. Sauté garlic in same skillet; push to one side.
3 Add frozen spinach block; cook, breaking up spinach as it thaws until spinach liquid has completely evaporated. Return ground beef to skillet with salt, rosemary, pepper, chicken broth, and water; stir to blend well.
4 Arrange 6 onion halves in a 13x9x2-inch baking dish. Spoon meat mixture over; arrange remaining onion halves, cut side up, on meat. Pour cream over all; cover.
5 Bake in moderate oven (375°) 50 minutes. Toss bread crumbs and melted butter or margarine together in a small bowl. Sprinkle over onions. Bake, uncovered, 10 minutes longer, or until bread crumbs are golden.

FOOD SAFETY TEMPERATURES

The USDA has set up this chart as a guide to the safest temperatures for holding various foods:

0°	*Safest temperature to store frozen foods. Do not store foods above 10°.*
32° to 40°	*The best temperature for holding foods in refrigerator.*
60° to 125°	*DANGER ZONE for all perishable foods.*
140° to 165°	*This is the temperature at which bacteria begin to be destroyed in cooking. Foods can be warmed at 140°, but not cooked.*
212°	*This is the temperature that a water-bath canner reaches and is safe for most jams, jellies, pickles and high-acid tomatoes.*
240°	*This is the temperature at which to process all low-acid vegetables, meats and poultry in a home-size pressure canner.*

Oven Beef Bounty

Ground beef and items from the pantry shelf combine for a hearty, inexpensive dinner

Bake at 350° for 1 hour.
Makes 8 servings

1 package (8 ounces) elbow macaroni
2 pounds ground beef
1 tablespoon vegetable oil
2 cans (1 pound each) mixed vegetables
1 envelope onion soup mix
¼ cup sifted all-purpose flour
1 teaspoon salt
¼ teaspoon pepper

1 Cook macaroni, following label directions; drain. Place in a 12-cup baking dish.
2 Shape ground beef into a large patty; brown in vegetable oil in a large frying pan 5 minutes on each side, then break up into chunks. Remove with a slotted spoon and add to macaroni.
3 Drain liquid from vegetables into a 4-cup

(continued)

measure; add water to make 3 cups; stir in onion soup mix. Add vegetables to meat mixture.
4 Pour drippings from frying pan, then measure 4 tablespoonfuls and return to pan. (If needed, add enough butter or margarine to measure 4 tablespoons.) Stir in flour, salt, and pepper. Cook, stirring constantly, until bubbly. Stir in onion-soup mixture; continue cooking and stirring until mixture thickens and boils 1 minute. Fold into meat and vegetables; cover baking dish tightly.
5 Bake in moderate oven (350°) 1 hour, or until bubbly.

Cabbage Burger Bake

An easy way to make popular cabbage rolls. Baking blends flavors perfectly

Bake at 400° for 1 hour.
Makes 6 generous servings

1 small head of cabbage (about 2 pounds)
6 slices of bacon
1 medium-size onion, chopped (½ cup)
1 cup uncooked regular rice
1 pound ground beef
½ pound ground fresh pork
1 teaspoon salt
⅛ teaspoon pepper
1 can (about 15 ounces) spaghetti sauce with mushrooms
3 cups water

1 Quarter and shred cabbage. (You should have about 8 cups.) Spread half in buttered shallow 12-cup baking dish.
2 Sauté bacon just until fat starts to cook out in large frying pan; remove; drain and set aside for Step 5.
3 Stir onion and rice into bacon drippings in frying pan; cook, stirring constantly, over medium heat, until onion is soft and rice is lightly browned. Spoon over cabbage in baking dish.
4 Shape ground beef and pork into a large patty in same frying pan. Brown 5 minutes on each side, then break up into chunks. Cook, stirring often, a few minutes longer, or until no pink remains. Spoon over rice mixture in baking dish; sprinkle with salt and pepper; top with remaining cabbage.
5 Heat spaghetti sauce with water to boiling in same frying pan. Pour slowly over cabbage, so sauce will seep into layers underneath. Top with bacon slices; cover.
6 Bake in hot oven (400°) 50 minutes, or until rice and cabbage are tender. Uncover; bake 10 minutes longer to crisp bacon.

Stuffed Pepper Cups

Big garden peppers are heaped with a peppy meat-and-bean filling, then baked

Bake at 350° for 30 minutes.
Makes 4 servings

4 large green peppers
1 pound ground beef
1 can (1 pound) pork and beans in tomato sauce
1 can (about 4 ounces) French-fried onion rings
½ cup catsup
1 teaspoon prepared mustard

1 Cut a thin slice from top of each pepper; scoop out seeds and membrane. Parboil peppers in a small amount of boiling salted water in a medium-size saucepan 10 minutes; drain well.
2 Shape ground beef into a large patty in a medium-size frying pan; brown 5 minutes on each side, then break up into small chunks.
3 Stir in pork and beans, half of the onions, catsup, and mustard. Spoon into pepper cups; place in a greased shallow baking pan.
4 Bake in moderate oven (350°) 20 minutes; place remaining onions on top, dividing evenly. Bake 10 minutes longer, or until onions are hot and crisp.

Tamale Bake

Give your menu a touch of the Southwest with cornmeal, a chili-tomato sauce, ripe olives, and Cheddar cheese

Bake at 400° for 1 hour.
Makes 6 servings

1 cup yellow cornmeal
1 pound ground beef
1 medium-size onion, chopped (½ cup)
½ cup chopped green pepper
1 envelope spaghetti-sauce mix
1 tablespoon chili powder
1 can (about 1 pound) tomatoes
1 can (7 ounces) pitted ripe olives, halved
1 cup grated Cheddar cheese (¼ pound)

1 Cook cornmeal, following label directions for cornmeal mush. Pour about half into an 8-cup shallow baking dish; spread evenly. Pour remaining into a greased pan, 9x5x3; chill.
2 Press ground beef into a large patty in large

frying pan; brown 5 minutes on each side; break up into chunks; push to one side.
3 Add onion and green pepper; sauté just until soft. Stir in spaghetti-sauce mix, chili powder, and tomatoes.
4 Heat to boiling, stirring constantly; remove from heat. Stir in olives and ¾ cup grated cheese. (Save remaining for Step 5.) Pour over cornmeal mush in baking dish. (This much can be done ahead; chill. Take from refrigerator 30 minutes before baking.)
5 Remove cornmeal mush from pan by turning upside down onto cutting board. Divide in half lengthwise, then cut each half into thirds; cut each piece diagonally to make 12 wedges. Arrange around edge of baking dish, sprinkle saved ¼ cup cheese on top.
6 Bake in hot oven (400°) 1 hour, or until bubbly-hot.

Oven Beef Bake

Popular ground meat blends with carrots, mushrooms, and macaroni.

Bake at 350° for 1 hour.
Makes 8 servings

1 package (8 ounces) elbow macaroni
1 can (1 pound) sliced carrots
1 can (6 ounces) sliced mushrooms
2 pounds ground beef
1 medium-size onion, chopped (½ cup)
2 cups thinly sliced celery
4 tablespoons (½ stick) butter or margarine
5 tablespoons all-purpose flour
1 teaspoon salt
¼ teaspoon pepper
1 can (10½ ounces) condensed beef broth

1 Cook macaroni, following label directions; drain.
2 Drain liquids from carrots and mushrooms into a 4-cup measure and set aside for Step 5. Combine vegetables with macaroni in a greased 12-cup baking dish.
3 Shape ground beef into a patty in a medium-size frying pan; brown 5 minutes on each side, then break up into small chunks. Stir into vegetable mixture in baking dish.
4 Sauté onion and celery in butter or margarine until golden in same frying pan; sprinkle with flour, salt, and pepper, then stir in. Cook, stirring constantly, just until bubbly.
5 Combine beef broth with saved vegetable juices; add water, if needed, to make 3 cups; stir into onion mixture. Continue cooking and stirring until sauce thickens and boils 1 minute. Pour over meat and vegetables; cover.
6 Bake in moderate oven (350°) 1 hour, or until sauce is bubbly. Garnish with rings of green pepper or about a cup of finely shredded lettuce, if you wish.

Lasagna Pie

America's favorite Italian dish appears here in a different guise. It's done in a pie plate.

Bake at 350° for 30 minutes.
Makes 8 servings

½ package lasagna noodles (from a 1-pound package)
1 pound ground round
1 small onion, chopped (¼ cup)
1 envelope lasagna sauce mix
1 can (1 pound) Italian tomatoes
1 can (8 ounces) tomato sauce with mushrooms
1 teaspoon sugar
½ cup water
1 pound ricotta cheese
2 packages (8 ounces each) mozzarella cheese, sliced
1 jar (3 ounces) grated Parmesan cheese
2 tablespoons chopped parsley

1 Cook lasagna noodles, following label directions; drain. Cool in a large bowl of cold water until ready to use.
2 Brown ground round in a large skillet; push to one side of pan. Sauté onion just until soft in same skillet. Drain off any excess fat.
3 Stir lasagna sauce mix, tomatoes, tomato sauce, sugar, and water into meat mixture in skillet. Heat to boiling; reduce heat; cover. Simmer 20 minutes.
4 Pour ½ cup of the prepared meat sauce into two 9-inch pie plates. Drain noodles; pat dry with paper toweling. Line the bottom of each plate with noodles, trimming noodles to fit the shape of the pie plate. Cover with a third of the ricotta cheese, meat sauce, mozzarella and Parmesan cheeses. Repeat to make 3 layers in both pie plates, ending with Parmesan cheese.
5 Bake in moderate oven (350°) 30 minutes, or until bubbly-hot. Let stand 10 minutes before serving. Garnish with parsley. Cut each pie into 4 wedges.

Our Favorite Lasagna

Among all the Lasagna recipes, this is a favorite. And, it's easy and quick to do

Bake at 350° for 30 minutes.
Makes 8 servings

½ pound sweet Italian sausages
½ pound ground beef
1 medium-size onion, chopped (½ cup)
1 clove garlic, minced
1 can (about 2 pounds) Italian tomatoes
1 envelope spaghetti-sauce mix
1 pound lasagna noodles
1 tablespoon vegetable oil
2 eggs
2 cups (1 pound) cream-style cottage cheese
2 packages (8 ounces each) sliced mozzarella or pizza cheese
½ cup grated Parmesan cheese

1 Squeeze sausages from casings; mix meat lightly with ground beef. Shape into a large patty in a frying pan; brown 5 minutes on each side, then break up into chunks; push to one side.
2 Stir in onion and garlic; sauté just until soft. Stir in tomatoes and spaghetti-sauce mix; simmer, stirring several times, 30 minutes, or until slightly thickened.
3 While sauce cooks, slide lasagna noodles, one at a time so as not to break, into a kettle of boiling salted water. Add salad oil; cook, following label directions. (Oil keeps noodles from sticking.) Cook, stirring often, 15 minutes, or just until tender. Drain; cover with cold water.
4 Beat eggs slightly; blend in cottage cheese.
5 Line bottom of a lightly oiled baking dish, 13x9x2, with a single layer of drained noodles. (Lift each strip separately from water and hold over kettle to drain.) Cover with a third each of cottage-cheese mixture, meat sauce, and mozzarella or pizza and Parmesan cheeses. Repeat to make two more layers of each. (Our picture shows the top layer of mozzarella cheese arranged in crisscross and triangle designs.)
6 Bake in moderate oven (350°) 30 minutes, or until bubbly hot. Garnish with a ripe-olive "flower" and parsley, if you wish. (To make olive "flower," cut a pitted ripe olive lengthwise into sixths; arrange, petal fashion, around a whole ripe olive.)

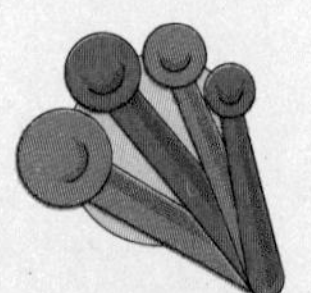

Hamburger Jubilee

Meat, noodles, vegetables, and a soup-sauce go into this hearty oven special

Bake at 350° for 40 minutes.
Makes 6 servings

1 pound ground beef
2 cups uncooked regular noodles
1 can (about 1 pound) tomatoes
2 cups shredded cabbage
1 cup sliced pared raw carrots
1 can (10¾ ounces) condensed cream of mushroom soup
1 cup water
1 teaspoon instant minced onion
½ teaspoon salt

1 Shape ground beef into a large patty in a large frying pan; brown 5 minutes on each side, then break up into small chunks. Spoon into an 8-cup baking dish.
2 Stir in remaining ingredients; cover.
3 Bake in moderate oven (350°) 40 minutes, or until noodles and vegetables are tender.

Oriental Pepper Pot

Ground beef, fish, and vegetables steam in a peppery-hot sauce for this unusual meal

Bake at 350° for 1 hour.
Makes 6 servings

1 pound ground beef
½ cup thinly sliced green onions
1 clove garlic, minced
1½ teaspoons sugar
¼ cup soy sauce
2 pounds fresh haddock fillets, cut in 2-inch pieces
1 large onion, chopped (1 cup)
6 large mushrooms, trimmed and sliced
4 medium-size carrots, pared and cut in 2-inch-long sticks
½ cup sliced celery
1½ teaspoons salt
1 teaspoon pepper
¼ teaspoon ground ginger
¾ cup water
1 egg
1 tablespoon butter or margarine

1 Mix ground beef with green onions, garlic, sugar, and 2 tablespoons of the soy sauce until

Our Favorite Lasagna is a great ground beef dinner, topped with golden mozzarella designs, to make it look as good as it tastes.

well blended in a bowl. (Remaining 2 tablespoons soy sauce are for Step 4.)
2 Spread half of the meat mixture evenly in a 12-cup baking dish; top with half each of the haddock, chopped onion, mushrooms, carrots, and celery.
3 Mix salt, pepper, and ginger in a cup; sprinkle half over layers in dish. Repeat with remaining ground-beef mixture, haddock, vegetables, and seasoning mixture.
4 Combine remaining 2 tablespoons soy sauce and water in a cup; pour over layers; cover tightly.
5 Bake in moderate oven (350°) 1 hour, or until haddock flakes easily and all vegetables are tender.
6 Just before serving, beat egg slightly in a cup; cook in butter or margarine, turning once, just until firm in a small frying pan. Cut in thin strips; mound in a petal design in center of baking dish.
7 Serve in soup plates or shallow bowls, for mixture is souplike.

Western Casserole

Cheesy meat balls bake in tomato soup along with beans and corn for a dish with the flavor of the old West

Bake at 350° for 1¼ hours.
Makes 4 servings

1 pound ground beef
½ cup grated American cheese
1½ teaspoons salt
1 tablespoon butter or margarine
¾ cup regular uncooked rice
1 medium size onion, chopped (½ cup)
1 can (10¾ ounces) condensed tomato soup
1 soup can of water
½ teaspoon leaf oregano, crumbled
¼ teaspoon dry mustard
1 can (about 1 pound) cut green beans, drained
1 can (12 ounces) whole-kernel corn

(continued)

1 Form beef, cheese, and 1 teaspoon salt lightly into 12 balls; brown in hot butter or margarine in frying pan; place in 8-cup baking dish; add rice.
2 Heat onion, soup, water, ½ teaspoon salt, oregano, and mustard to boiling; pour over meat balls; arrange vegetables around edge; cover.
3 Bake in moderate oven (350°) 1¼ hours, or until rice is tender.

Mandarin Beef

Sauté meat quickly, the Oriental way, then combine with soy-seasoned sauce and bake

Bake at 350° for 1 hour and 10 minutes.
Makes 6 to 8 servings

2 pounds round steak or boneless beef chuck
Instant unseasoned meat tenderizer
¼ cup peanut oil or vegetable oil
1 large onion, chopped (1 cup)
2 cups sliced celery
2 cans (3 or 4 ounces each) sliced mushrooms
1 can (10¾ ounces) condensed cream of chicken soup
½ cup water
¼ cup soy sauce
2 cups shredded Chinese cabbage
¼ cup toasted slivered almonds (from a 5-ounce can)

1 Moisten meat and sprinkle with tenderizer, following label directions; cut in 2-inch-long strips about ½ inch thick.
2 Brown, a few at a time, in part of the peanut oil or vegetable oil in a large frying pan, adding more oil as needed; spoon into an 8-cup baking dish. Sauté onion just until soft in drippings in frying pan; add with celery to meat.
3 Stir mushrooms and liquid, soup, water, and soy sauce into frying pan; heat to boiling; pour over meat mixture; cover.
4 Bake in moderate oven (350°) 1 hour, or until meat is tender; uncover. Place shredded cabbage on top; cover again.
5 Bake 10 minutes longer, or just until cabbage wilts. Just before serving, sprinkle with almonds and serve over rice, if you wish.

Steak Piquant

Man-size chunks of beef bake with noodles, limas, and tomatoes in this colorful entrée

Bake at 350° for 30 minutes.
Makes 6 Servings

2 pounds lean round steak or beef chuck, cut into 1-inch cubes
2 tablespoons vegetable oil
½ cup water
2 beef-bouillon cubes
1½ teaspoons salt
½ teaspoon ground cardamom
¼ teaspoon pepper
1 tablespoon lemon juice
1 package (8 ounces) noodles
1 package (10 ounces) frozen baby lima beans
3 medium-size tomatoes, cut into wedges
1 teaspoon sugar
1 tablespoon finely chopped parsley

1 Brown beef cubes in vegetable oil in large frying pan. Stir in water, bouillon cubes, salt, cardamom, pepper, and lemon juice. Cover; simmer 20 to 30 minutes, or until meat is tender.
2 Cook noodles, following label directions; drain; place in greased 12-cup baking dish.
3 Cook lima beans, following label directions; drain; spoon over noodles to make a ring around edge of baking dish.
4 Spoon meat in middle, then pour juices over all. Arrange tomato wedges, overlapping, on top of lima beans; sprinkle with sugar and salt and pepper, if desired; cover.
5 Bake in moderate oven (350°) 30 minutes to blend flavors. Sprinkle parsley over top just before serving.

Ravioli Bake

A little ground beef adds extra heartiness to canned cheese ravioli

Bake at 375° for 30 minutes.
Makes 4 generous servings

1 medium-size onion, chopped (½ cup)
1 large green pepper, halved, seeded, and cut in squares
1 tablespoon butter or margarine
½ pound ground beef
¼ cup sliced ripe olives
1 teaspoon leaf basil, crumbled

1 tablespoon bottled steak sauce
2 cans (15 ounces each) cheese ravioli in tomato sauce

1 Sauté onion and green pepper in butter or margarine until soft in a large frying pan; push to one side.
2 Shape ground beef into a patty in same pan. Brown 5 minutes on each side, then break up into small chunks; stir in olives, basil, and steak sauce.
3 Place half of the ravioli in a 6-cup baking dish; top with meat mixture, then remaining ravioli.
4 Bake in moderate oven (375°) 30 minutes, or until bubbly.

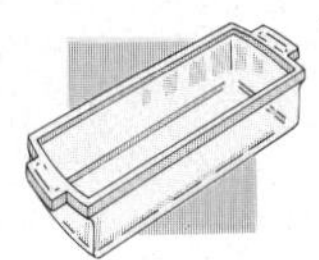

Chili Tamale Pie

A casserole with a South-of-the-Border touch with its chili tomato sauce, tamales, and beans

Bake at 350°
Makes 6 servings

¾ cup cornmeal
3 cups water
2 tablespoons butter or margarine
1 teaspoon salt
2 tablespoons vegetable oil or olive oil
1 large onion, chopped (1 cup)
1 clove of garlic, minced
1 pound ground beef
2 cans (about 1 pound each) baked pea or kidney beans
1 can (8 ounces) tomato sauce
2 teaspoons chili powder
1 teaspoon salt
⅛ teaspoon pepper
1 can (about 1 pound) tamales, drained and cut in half

1 Blend cornmeal and ½ cup water in small bowl until smooth.
2 Bring remaining 2½ cups water, butter or margarine, and salt to boiling in medium-size saucepan; stirring constantly, gradually add cornmeal mixture.
3 Cook, stirring often, until thick; cover and continue to cook over very low heat 10 minutes; remove from heat; save for Step 6.
4 While cornmeal cooks, heat oil in large frying pan; add onion and garlic; sauté over low heat about 5 minutes, or just until tender; add ground beef; cook until brown, breaking meat up with a fork as it cooks.
5 Stir in beans, tomato sauce, chili powder, salt, and pepper; heat to boiling; reduce heat; simmer 20 minutes to blend flavors.
6 Line bottom and sides of baking dish, 12x8x2, with cooked cornmeal; pour hot chili mixture on top of cornmeal; top with halved tamales.
7 Bake according to directions in Step 8, or cool, then keep in refrigerator until 1½ hours before serving time and bake according to directions in Step 8A.
8 Bake at once in moderate oven (350° F.) about 40 minutes, or until filling is bubbly-hot.
8A Remove chilled casserole from refrigerator; let stand 30 minutes at room temperature; then bake in moderate oven (350°) for 50 to 60 minutes, or until filling is bubbly-hot. Serve with grated cheese, if desired.

Chuck Wagon Beef Casserole

Beef and bacon, plus four vegetables, bake in a tarragon-seasoned sauce

Bake at 350° for 30 minutes.
Makes 6 servings

2 cups cubed cooked beef
3 tablespoons all-purpose flour
½ pound bacon (about 12 slices), cut in 1-inch pieces
1 can (10½ ounces) condensed beef broth
1 teaspoon paprika
1 teaspoon leaf tarragon, crumbled
1 can (about 1 pound) red kidney beans, drained
1 can (about 1 pound) chick peas, drained
1 can (16 ounces) whole-kernel corn, drained
1 cup chopped celery

1 Shake beef cubes with flour in a paper bag to coat evenly.
2 Sauté bacon until crisp in a large frying pan; remove and drain on paper toweling. Pour off all fat, then return 2 tablespoonfuls to pan.
3 Add beef cubes and brown; remove. Stir any remaining flour into drippings in pan, then stir in beef broth, paprika and tarragon. Cook, stirring constantly, until mixture thickens and boils 1 minute.
4 Spoon beans, chick peas, corn and celery into a shallow 8-cup baking dish; top with browned beef cubes and bacon; pour sauce over.
5 Bake in moderate oven (350°) 30 minutes, or until bubbly-hot.

French Bean Bake

A thrifty, peasant-style dish using leftover roast beef with beans and onions

Bake at 375° for 30 minutes.
Makes 4 servings

2 cups cubed roast beef
2 tablespoons butter or margarine
½ teaspoon salt
½ teaspoon leaf thyme, crumbled
⅛ teaspoon pepper
1 cup apple cider
2 cans (1 pound each) white kidney beans, drained
1 can (1 pound) small boiled onions, drained
½ cup chopped parsley

1 Brown beef in butter or margarine in a medium-size frying pan; stir in salt, thyme, pepper and cider; heat to boiling.
2 Spoon into a 6-cup baking dish; stir in beans and onions; cover.
3 Bake in moderate oven (375°) 30 minutes, or until bubbly-hot. Sprinkle with chopped parsley and serve with French bread, if you wish.

Family Steak

Meat bubbles away in a zesty tomato sauce for a savory Old World flavor

Bake at 350° for 1½ hours.
Makes 6 servings

3 pounds chuck steak, cut about 1½ inches thick (often labeled California Roast)
1 envelope (2¼ ounces) spaghetti-sauce mix with tomato
2 cans (about 1 pound each) small whole potatoes, drained
2 cans (about 1 pound each) sliced carrots, drained

1 Brown steak slowly 10 minutes on each side in large heavy frying pan with heat-proof handle or in Dutch oven.
2 While meat browns, prepare spaghetti-sauce mix with water, following label directions; pour over meat; cover.
3 Bake in moderate oven (350°) 1 hour. Place potatoes and carrots in separate piles on top of meat; spoon some of the sauce over each; cover. Bake 30 minutes longer, or until meat is tender.
4 Place meat at one side of heated serving platter; arrange potatoes and carrots around edge. Garnish with parsley, if you wish. Pass sauce in separate bowl to spoon over meat.

Mushroom Steak Bake

Thick chuck roast makes its own rich gravy as it bubbles in foil

Bake at 350° for 3 hours,
then broil for 5 minutes.
Makes 8 servings

1 envelope (2 to a package) mushroom soup mix
1 tablespoon instant minced onion
1 four-pound chuck beef roast, cut 1½ inches thick

1 Combine dry soup mix and onion on a sheet of heavy foil, about 24x18. Roll roast in mixture to coat well, then wrap loosely, sealing edges well. Place on a cookie sheet for easy handling.
2 Bake in moderate oven (350°) 3 hours. Remove from oven; reset temperature control to BROIL.
3 Slit foil across top and fold back, being careful not to let gravy run out. Broil roast 5 minutes, or until top is brown.
4 Carve into ¼-inch-thick slices; serve with gravy from foil package.

Country Casserole Steak

Jumbo steak and sliced smoky sausages bake with vegetables and fruit, then blend with hot macaroni

Bake at 350° for 2 hours.
Makes 4 servings

1 boneless chuck beef steak, weighing about 2 pounds
2 tablespoons all-purpose flour
1 teaspoon salt
¼ teaspoon pepper
1 large onion, peeled, sliced and separated into rings
1 cup sliced pared carrots
1 cup sliced celery
1 medium-size tart apple or pear, pared, quartered, cored and sliced

1 package (6 ounces) smoked sausage links, sliced ½ inch thick
1 cup water
¼ cup catsup
½ cup chopped parsley
1 cup elbow macaroni (half an 8-ounce package)

1 Trim excess fat from steak. Rub steak with mixture of flour, salt and pepper. Brown in a large heavy frying pan over medium heat or in an electric skillet.
2 Mix onion, carrots, celery and apple or pear in a greased 12-cup baking dish; top with browned steak and sausage slices.
3 Stir water, catsup and ¼ cup of the parsley into drippings in pan; heat to boiling; pour over meats; cover. (Set remaining ¼ cup parsley aside for Step 6.)
4 Bake in moderate oven (350°) 2 hours, or until steak is very tender.
5 While meat mixture bakes, cook macaroni, following label directions; drain.
6 Remove steak to a cutting board; cut into ½-inch-thick slices. Skim all fat from mixture in baking dish; stir in macaroni and remaining ¼ cup parsley. Arrange sliced meat on top.

VEAL

Sweet-and-Spicy Meat

Leftovers were never better! Slice meat, then glaze with a soy-rich sauce

Bake at 400° about 30 minutes.
Makes 6 servings

2 tablespoons vegetable oil
2 tablespoons soy sauce
2 tablespoons molasses
1 tablespoon cider vinegar
1 small onion, chopped (¼ cup)
12 slices cooked pork, veal, lamb, ham or beef or a combination

1 Combine vegetable oil, soy sauce, molasses, vinegar, and onion in small saucepan. Heat to boiling, then simmer, uncovered, 8 to 10 minutes, or until reduced by about half.
2 Arrange meat slices, slightly overlapping, in large shallow baking pan; brush with about ⅓ of sauce mixture.
3 Bake in hot oven (400°), brushing 2 or 3 times with remaining sauce and pan drippings, 30 minutes, or until heated through and lightly glazed.

Continental Veal Casserole

So easy to make with canned chicken gravy

Bake at 375° for 1 hour and 45 minutes.
Makes 12 servings

1½ pounds ground veal
¾ pound ground beef
1 cup coarse soft bread crumbs (2 slices)
2 eggs, beaten
1 teaspoon salt
½ teaspoon ground mace
¼ teaspoon pepper
2 cans (about 1 pound each) whole white onions, drained
2 cans (10½ ounces each) chicken gravy
1 cup uncooked regular rice
1 package (10 ounces) frozen peas
1 cup (8-ounce carton) dairy sour cream
½ cup toasted slivered almonds

1 Mix veal, beef, bread crumbs, eggs, salt, mace, and pepper lightly with a fork in large bowl; shape into 48 small balls.
2 Layer meat balls and drained onions in a 16-cup casserole (or use 2 eight-cup ones); pour chicken gravy over; cover.
3 Bake in moderate oven (375°) 1 hour and 15 minutes, or until mixture is bubbling in center and meat is done.
4 While casserole bakes, cook rice, following label directions; drain; place frozen peas on top of rice in saucepan.
5 Measure out ½ cup peas for Step 7; stir remaining peas and sour cream into rice, then stir all into casserole.
6 Bake, uncovered, 30 minutes longer, or until bubbly-hot.
7 Cook the saved ½ cup peas in small amount boiling salted water in small saucepan just until tender; drain; sprinkle over bubbling casserole; top with a ring of toasted slivered almonds.

Veal Taormina

Italian food fans will go for this zesty combination of meat and eggplant in tomato-rich sauce

Bake at 350° for 40 minutes.
Makes 6 to 8 servings

2 eggs
1 cup fine dry bread crumbs
1 large eggplant, pared and sliced ¼ inch thick
¾ cup vegetable oil
1 pound ground veal
3 cans (8 ounces each) tomato sauce
2 teaspoons sugar
1 teaspoon leaf oregano, crumbled
½ teaspoon leaf basil, crumbled
½ teaspoon salt
½ cup grated Parmesan cheese
1 package (8 ounces) sliced mozzarella or pizza cheese, cut into triangles

1 Beat eggs slightly in a pie plate; sprinkle bread crumbs in a second pie plate. Dip eggplant slices into egg, then into crumbs to coat well.
2 Brown, a few at a time, in part of the vegetable oil in a large frying pan, adding more oil as needed; drain slices on paper toweling. Wipe out frying pan.
3 Shape veal into a large patty in same frying pan; brown, adding more oil, if needed, 5 minutes on each side, then break up into chunks. Stir in tomato sauce, sugar, oregano, basil, and salt; simmer 10 minutes.
4 Layer one third each of the eggplant slices, meat sauce, Parmesan cheese, and mozzarella triangles into a greased baking dish, 13x9x2. Repeat to make 2 more layers of each, arranging the remaining mozzarella triangles in a pretty pattern on top.
5 Bake in moderate oven (350°) 40 minutes, or until bubbly-hot and cheese melts slightly. Garnish with ripe olive flowers, if you wish. To make, cut a slice from one end of each of 2 large pitted ripe olives for flower centers; slice remaining into thin strips. Arrange strips, petal fashion, around slices.
Hostess note—Casserole can be made ahead and chilled. When ready to bake, place in a cold oven; set heat control at moderate (350°). Bake 45 to 60 minutes, or until bubbly-hot.

Veal Risotto

Rice and meat are lightly seasoned with curry for this inviting one-dish meal

Bake at 350° for 1 hour.
Makes 8 servings

2 pounds cubed veal shoulder
2 tablespoons vegetable oil
1 tablespoon curry powder
2 cups uncooked regular rice
2 packages (10 ounces each) frozen mixed vegetables, thawed
2 tablespoons instant minced onion
2 envelopes instant chicken broth
1½ teaspoons salt
5 cups water
2 canned whole pimientos, drained and halved

1 Trim any fat from veal; brown cubes in vegetable oil in a large frying pan. Stir in curry powder; cook, stirring constantly, 1 minute.
2 While meat browns, mix rice, frozen vegetables, and onion in a greased 12-cup baking dish. Arrange meat in a single layer on top.
3 Stir chicken broth, salt, and water into same frying pan; heat to boiling; pour over meat and vegetables; cover.
4 Bake in moderate oven (350°) 1 hour, or until meat and rice are tender and liquid is absorbed. Arrange pimientos on top.

Hungarian Veal

Mild-flavor veal and autumn vegetables bubble temptingly in a creamy-rich gravy

Bake at 350° for 25 minutes.
Makes 6 servings

1½ pounds veal shoulder, cut in cubes
¼ cup sifted all-purpose flour
2 teaspoons salt
⅛ teaspoon pepper
2 tablespoons vegetable oil
1½ cups water
12 small white onions, peeled
1 small eggplant, pared and diced
1 cup dairy sour cream
1 teaspoon paprika
2 cans (2¼ ounces each) shoestring potatoes

1 Shake veal in flour, 1 teaspoon salt, and pepper in paper bag to coat well. (Save remaining salt for Step 2.)

Continental Veal Bake is a prepare-now, eat later casserole that spares the cook.

2 Brown quickly in vegetable oil in large frying pan; stir in water and remaining teaspoon of salt, then add onions and eggplant. Cover; simmer 30 minutes, or until onions are tender.
3 Stir in sour cream and paprika; spoon mixture into an 8-cup baking dish; sprinkle potatoes evenly over top.
4 Bake in moderate oven (350°) 25 minutes, or until meat is tender.

Continental Veal Bake

A variation that will please all who love veal cooked to perfection

Bake at 350° for 1 hour.
Makes 6 servings

1 package (8 ounces) regular noodles
1½ pounds cube veal steaks
½ cup sifted all-purpose flour
1 teaspoon salt
⅛ teaspoon pepper
2 tablespoons butter or margarine
1 chicken-bouillon cube
2 cups water
1 cup dairy sour cream
2 tablespoons chopped parsley
½ teaspoon grated lemon rind
2 tablespoons grated Parmesan cheese
1 package (10 ounces) frozen green peas and onions

1 Cook noodles in boiling salted water in a kettle, following label directions; drain; return to kettle.
2 While noodles cook, cut veal steaks into quarters. Mix flour, salt, and pepper in a pie plate. Dip veal into flour mixture to coat both sides.
3 Brown quickly, a few pieces at a time, in butter or margarine in a large frying pan; remove and set aside for Step 6.
4 Stir any remaining flour mixture and bouillon

(continued)

cube into drippings in frying pan; stir in water slowly. Cook, stirring constantly and scraping browned bits from bottom and side of pan, until sauce thickens and boils 1 minute.
5 Stir a small amount of hot sauce into sour cream in a medium-size bowl, then stir in remaining sauce, parsley, and lemon rind. Pour over noodles in kettle; toss lightly to mix.
6 Spoon noodles into a buttered shallow 8-cup baking dish; sprinkle with Parmesan cheese. Arrange veal, overlapping slices, on top of noodles. Cover and chill.
7 One hour before serving time, place covered casserole in a cold oven; set heat control at moderate (350°). Bake 45 minutes. Uncover, and, if noodles seem dry (they take up sauce on standing), pour about a half cup of milk over. Gently lift noodles with a fork so milk will seep to bottom. Bake, uncovered, 15 minutes longer, or until bubbly-hot in middle.
8 While casserole bakes, cook peas and onions, following label directions. Spoon on top of noodles just before serving.

HAM AND PORK

Porkie Pie

Ground pork patties are topped with mashed sweet potatoes and baked for an extra-special entree

Bake at 400° for 20 minutes.
Makes 4 servings

4 medium-size sweet potatoes or yams
2 tablespoons butter or margarine
1¾ teaspoons salt
1½ teaspoons cinnamon-sugar
1 pound ground fresh pork
Dash of pepper
2 tablespoons flour
1½ cups water

1 Cook sweet potatoes or yams, covered, in boiling salted water in a large saucepan 30 minutes, or until tender; drain. Cool until easy to handle; peel.
2 Mash potatoes slightly in a large bowl, then beat in butter or margarine, ½ teaspoon of the salt, and cinnamon-sugar until smooth and fluffy.
3 While potatoes cook, mix ground pork with 1 teaspoon of the remaining salt and pepper. Shape into 16 two-inch patties.
4 Brown patties slowly, a few at a time, in a medium-size frying pan; place in a shallow 6-cup baking dish.
5 Pour all drippings from frying pan, then measure 2 tablespoonfuls and return to pan. (If needed, add enough butter or margarine to measure 2 tablespoons.) Blend in flour and remaining ¼ teaspoon salt; cook, stirring constantly, until bubbly. Stir in water; continue cooking and stirring until gravy thickens and boils 1 minute. Pour over meat in baking dish; spread mashed sweet potatoes over all.
6 Bake in hot oven (400°) 20 minutes, or until bubbly.

Summer Ham Scallop

For a satisfying meal, serve with a big green salad and crusty bread

Bake at 350° for 1 hour.
Makes 8 servings

1 one-pound canned ham
1 package (about 4 ounces) potato chips
2 cans (16 ounces each) whole-kernel corn
2 cans (1 pound each) small boiled onions, drained
1 cup thinly sliced celery
2 hard-cooked eggs, shelled and diced
¼ cup chopped parsley
4 tablespoons (½ stick) butter or margarine
4 tablespoons all-purpose flour
1 envelope instant beef broth
OR: 1 beef-flavor bouillon cube
⅛ teaspoon pepper
1 tall can (14½ ounces) evaporated milk

1 Cut ham into ¼-inch-thick slices. Pick out four of the largest center slices and halve each diagonally for garnish; dice remaining.
2 Set aside 8 large potato chips for garnish; crumble remaining coarsely. (There should be about 2 cups.)
3 Drain liquid from corn into a cup; combine corn with onions, diced ham, crumbled potato chips, celery, diced eggs, and parsley in a greased 12-cup baking dish.
4 Melt butter or margarine in a medium-size saucepan; stir in flour, beef broth or bouillon cube, and pepper; cook, stirring constantly, until bubbly.

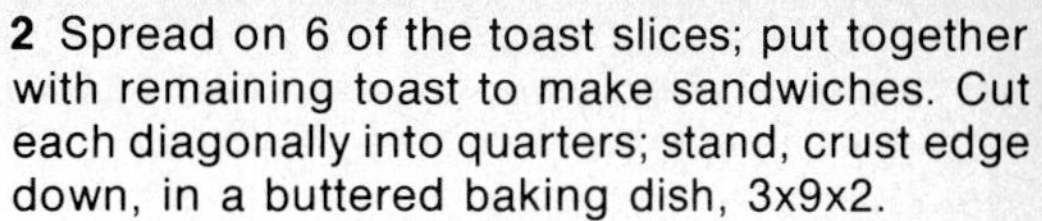

5 Add enough corn liquid to evaporated milk to make 2 cups; stir into flour mixture in saucepan. Continue cooking and stirring, crushing bouillon cube, if used, with a spoon, until sauce thickens and boils 1 minute. Pour over meat and vegetables; toss lightly with a fork to mix.
6 Arrange ham triangles in a circle on top; tuck saved potato chips between ham slices; cover.
7 Bake in moderate oven (350°) 1 hour, or until sauce is bubbly. Just before serving, garnish with sprigs of parsley, if you wish.

Ham-and-Swiss Sandwich Puff

Toasted ham and cheese sandwiches are baked in a custard sauce; serve them for supper or luncheon

Bake at 325° for 35 minutes.
Makes 6 to 8 servings

2 cups ground cooked ham (about 1 pound)
2 cups grated Swiss cheese (½ pound)
½ cup mayonnaise or salad dressing
1 teaspoon prepared mustard
12 slices white bread, toasted
6 eggs
2¼ cups milk

1 Combine ham and cheese in a medium-size bowl. (Tip: Putting both through a food chopper, using coarse blade, speeds the job.) Blend in mayonnaise or salad dressing and mustard.
2 Spread on 6 of the toast slices; put together with remaining toast to make sandwiches. Cut each diagonally into quarters; stand, crust edge down, in a buttered baking dish, 3x9x2.
3 Beat eggs slightly with milk in a medium-size bowl; pour over sandwiches. Cover and chill at least 4 hours, or overnight.
4 Bake in slow oven (325°) 35 minutes, or just until custard sets. Garnish with parsley, if you wish. To serve, cut between sandwiches; lift onto serving plates with a wide spatula.

Ham-and-Potato Scallop

Always popular with meat-and-potato fans—and this one goes together quickly

Bake at 350° for 40 minutes.
Makes 4 servings

4 cups sliced, peeled, cooked potatoes
2 cups cubed cooked ham
1 can (1 pound) small boiled onions, drained
2 cups milk
3 tablespoons instant-type flour
2 tablespoons butter or margarine
½ teaspoon salt
⅛ teaspoon pepper

1 Make two layers each of the potato slices, ham, and onions in a shallow 8-cup baking dish.
2 Combine milk, flour, butter or margarine, salt, and pepper in a small saucepan; cook, stirring constantly, until sauce thickens and boils 1 minute; pour over layers.
3 Bake in moderate oven (350°) 40 minutes, or until bubbly hot. Sprinkle with finely cut chives, if you wish.

When the occasion calls for something special, try bubbling **Ham-and-Swiss Sandwich Puffs.**

Wikiwiki Ham Bake

First word in its name means "hurry up" and this dish is just that—a good stand-by when time is short

Bake at 400° for 20 minutes.
Makes 6 servings

1 slice ready-to-eat ham, cut about ¾ inch thick
1 can (1 pound, 4 ounces) pineapple chunks
½ cup firmly packed brown sugar
1 can (about 1 pound) whole sweet potatoes
12 marshmallows

1 Cut ham into 6 serving-size pieces; brown in large frying pan.
2 Drain syrup from pineapple into 2-cup measure (there will be about 1 cup); stir in brown sugar until dissolved; pour over ham; heat to boiling.
3 Pile ham in middle of an 8-cup baking dish; arrange sweet potatoes around edge. Tuck pineapple chunks in between potatoes; pour hot syrup over.
4 Bake in hot oven (400°) 15 minutes; remove from oven and place marshmallows around edge; bake 5 minutes longer, or until marshmallows are toasty-brown.

Country Style Pork Pie

The combination of cabbage, mashed potatoes, eggs, and brown gravy turns this into a wholesome delight

Bake at 400° for 15 minutes.
Makes 4 servings

1 small head cabbage (about 1 pound)
4 tablespoons (½ stick) butter or margarine
1 teaspoon salt
¼ teaspoon pepper
4 cups prepared instant mashed potatoes
1 cup diced cooked pork
1 can (10½ ounces) brown gravy with onions
4 hard-cooked eggs, diced
¼ cup chopped parsley

1 Trim cabbage and shred (you will have about 5 cups). Cook in lightly salted water in a large saucepan for 5 minutes, or just until crisply tender; drain well. Toss with 2 tablespoons of the butter or margarine, salt, and pepper.
2 Fold prepared potatoes into cabbage. Spoon over bottom and sides of a buttered shallow 8-cup baking dish.
3 Melt remaining 2 tablespoons butter or margarine in a small skillet; sauté pork 1 minute; add gravy; heat to boiling; remove from heat. Carefully mix in eggs and parsley. Spoon into potato-lined dish.
4 Bake in hot oven (400°) for 15 minutes, or until bubbly-hot.

Pork and Sweet Potato Bake

The tang of sauerkraut and the sweetness of apricot jam, plus the spices, add up to a blend of sweet-sour flavors for pork chops

Bake at 350° for 1 hour.
Makes 6 servings

6 loin, rib, or shoulder pork chops, cut ½ inch thick
2 cans (1 pound each) sauerkraut
⅛ teaspoon dry mustard
¼ cup water
6 raw medium-size sweet potatoes, pared and sliced lengthwise
½ teaspoon salt
⅛ teaspoon pepper
½ cup apricot jam
¼ teaspoon ginger

1 Trim any excess fat from chops with sharp knife.
2 Heat large frying pan; rub with piece of cut-off fat; brown chops on both sides in pan; save for Step 4.
3 Spread undrained sauerkraut in bottom of 2-quart baking dish; sprinkle with dry mustard and water.
4 Arrange sweet-potato slices around edge; place browned chops in center; sprinkle with salt and pepper.
5 Combine apricot jam and ginger; spread over sweet potatoes.
6 Bake, covered, in moderate oven (350°) 1 hour, or until chops and potatoes are tender when tested with a fork.

Baked Pork Chops and Noodles

Pork chops and noodles bake in seasoned tomato sauce for a family-style dinner

Bake at 350° about 1 hour and 10 minutes.
Makes 4 servings

4 loin, rib, or shoulder pork chops, cut ¾ inch thick
2 cans (about 1 pound each) tomatoes
1 medium-size onion, chopped (½ cup)
2 teaspoons salt
1 teaspoon sugar
½ teaspoon leaf marjoram, crumbled
1 bay leaf
⅛ teaspoon pepper
1 package (8 ounces) noodles
4 thin onion slices
8 green-pepper strips

1 Trim excess fat from chops; broil on both sides in large heavy frying pan; drain on paper toweling.
2 Mix tomatoes, onion, salt, sugar, marjoram, bay leaf, and pepper in large bowl.
3 Place dry noodles in 8-cup baking dish; pour tomato mixture over; arrange pork chops on top; garnish each with an onion slice and 2 green-pepper strips; cover tightly with aluminum foil.
4 Bake in moderate oven (350°) for 1 hour; remove cover; bake 10 minutes longer, or until chops are tender.

Bring out the luau and festoon the table with flowers when serving up **Wikiwiki Ham Bake.**

Chopstick Pork

Crisp-cooked vegetables and mellow fruits in a sweet-sour sauce frame soy-seasoned pork

Bake at 350° for 30 minutes.
Makes 6 servings

3 cups cubed roast pork
4 tablespoons soy sauce
6 medium-size carrots, scraped and sliced ½ inch thick
2 medium-size green peppers, halved, seeded, and cut in 1-inch pieces
1 can (1 pound) sliced cling peaches
3 tablespoons vegetable oil
1 large onion, chopped (1 cup)
1 can (about 14 ounces) chicken broth
¼ cup cider vinegar
3 tablespoons cornstarch
3 tablespoons water
3 medium-size bananas
1 can (3 ounces) Chinese fried noodles

1 Combine pork and soy sauce in a medium-size bowl; toss lightly to mix; let stand to season while cooking the vegetables.
2 Cook carrots in boiling salted water in a medium-size saucepan 15 minutes, or just until crisply tender; drain. Parboil green peppers in boiling salted water in a small saucepan 5 minutes; drain. Set both carrots and peppers aside for Step 6.
3 Drain syrup from peaches into a 1-cup measure; set peaches aside for Step 6.
4 Drain pork, saving soy sauce in a cup. Brown pork in salad oil in a large frying pan; remove and set aside for Step 6. Stir onion into drippings in pan; sauté just until soft. Stir in ½ cup of the peach syrup, chicken broth, vinegar, and saved soy sauce.
5 Smooth cornstarch and water to a paste in a cup; stir into onion mixture; cook, stirring constantly, until mixture thickens and boils 3 minutes. Remove from heat.
6 Peel bananas; halve lengthwise and cut into 2-inch pieces. Arrange with cooked carrots, green peppers, and peach slices in separate mounds in a shallow 8-cup baking dish; pile browned pork in center; pour hot onion sauce evenly over top.
7 Sprinkle noodles between mounds; top with a ring of water-chestnut slices, if you wish.
8 Bake, uncovered, in moderate oven (350°) 30 minutes, or until bubbly-hot in center.

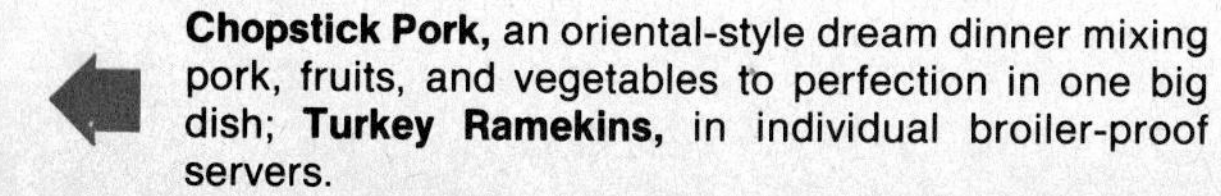
Chopstick Pork, an oriental-style dream dinner mixing pork, fruits, and vegetables to perfection in one big dish; **Turkey Ramekins,** in individual broiler-proof servers.

Chinese Chops

Pineapple and sweet-sour sauce give these chops a traditional Oriental touch

Bake at 350° for 1 hour.
Makes 6 servings

6 loin or rib pork chops, cut ½ inch thick
½ teaspoon salt
1 cup uncooked regular rice
2½ cups boiling water
1 tablespoon butter or margarine
½ small green pepper, halved, seeded and cut in thin strips
1 can (8¼ ounces) pineapple chunks
1 envelope (2 ounces) sweet-sour sauce mix

1 Trim all fat from chops. Sauté a few of the trimmings in a large frying pan; remove and discard. Place chops in drippings; sauté slowly, turning once, until brown; sprinkle with salt.
2 Place rice in a shallow 10-cup baking dish; stir in boiling water and butter or margarine. Place chops in a single layer on top; cover.
3 Bake in moderate oven (350°) 50 minutes; uncover.
4 While chops bake, sauté green pepper until soft in remaining drippings in frying pan.
5 Drain syrup from pineapple into a 2-cup measure; add water to make 1¼ cups. Sprinkle sauce mix over green pepper in pan; stir in pineapple liquid. Heat, stirring constantly, to boiling. Stir in pineapple; simmer, stirring constantly, 1 minute. Pour over chops.
6 Bake 10 minutes longer to blend the flavors.

Dinner Ham Casserole

Meat, vegetables and gravy cook in one dish. Make ahead to bake at mealtime

Bake at 350° for 30 minutes.
Makes 4 servings

1 package (10 ounces) frozen baby lima beans
2 medium-size carrots, scraped and sliced thin (about 1 cup)
1 medium-size cucumber, pared, quartered lengthwise and cubed
3 cups diced cooked lean ham (about 1 pound)
1 medium-size onion, chopped (½ cup)
2 tablespoons butter or margarine
1 can (10¾ ounces) condensed cream of celery soup
⅔ cup milk
⅛ teaspoon pepper
1 package (4 ounces) corn chips, crushed

(continued)

1 Cook lima beans and carrots together, following label directions for limas; add cucumber for last 2 minutes' cooking; drain.
2 Sauté ham and onion in butter or margarine in large frying pan 5 minutes, or until onion is softened. Stir in soup, milk and pepper; heat, stirring constantly, just until blended.
3 Pour into a buttered 6-cup casserole; stir in cooked vegetables; sprinkle crushed corn chips over.
4 Bake in moderate oven (350°) 30 minutes, or until bubbly-hot.
Note—If made in the morning and chilled, take casserole from refrigerator and let stand at room temperature for 30 minutes before putting into oven to bake.

Alabama Ham Bake

Under a jumbo puffy-golden pancake are layers of mellow ham, sweet potatoes, and apples

Bake at 375° for 1 hour.
Makes 6 servings

2 medium-size sweet potatoes, pared and sliced thin
3 medium-size pears, pared, quartered, cored and sliced
3 cups diced cooked ham (about 1 pound)
3 tablespoons brown sugar
½ teaspoon salt
¼ teaspoon pepper
¼ teaspoon curry powder
⅓ cup apple cider
1 cup pancake mix
½ teaspoon dry mustard
1 cup milk
2 tablespoons melted butter or margarine

1 Layer half each of the sweet potatoes, pears and ham in an 8-cup baking dish.
2 Mix brown sugar, salt, pepper and curry powder in a cup; sprinkle half on top of layers in baking dish. Repeat with remaining sweet potatoes, pears, ham and seasonings; pour apple cider over; cover.
3 Bake in moderate oven (375°) 40 minutes, or until sweet potatoes are tender.
4 While ham mixture bakes, combine pancake mix, mustard, milk and melted butter or margarine in a medium-size bowl, blending well to make a thin batter; pour over hot ham mixture.
5 Bake, uncovered, 20 minutes longer, or until pancake topping is puffed and golden.

Golden Gate Ham Rollups

Ham slices are wrapped around herb stuffing, then glazed and baked with peach halves

Bake at 350° for 40 minutes.
Makes 8 servings

2 tablespoons minced onion
2 tablespoons butter or margarine
¾ cup water
2 cups ready-mix bread stuffing (half an 8-ounce package)
8 large thin slices cooked ham (about 1½ pounds)
1 can (1 pound, 13 ounces) peach halves
½ cup orange marmalade
1 tablespoon cider vinegar
½ teaspoon dry mustard

1 Sauté onion in butter or margarine just until softened in medium-size saucepan. Add water; heat to boiling. Remove from heat; stir in bread stuffing.
2 Spoon about ¼ cup stuffing onto each ham slice; roll up; fasten with wooden picks, if needed. Place, seam side down, in single layer in greased large shallow baking pan.
3 Drain peach halves, saving ¼ cup syrup for next step. Place peaches, rounded side up, in baking pan with ham rolls.
4 Combine saved ¼ cup peach syrup, orange marmalade, vinegar and mustard in small saucepan; heat, stirring constantly, just until bubbly. Brush ham rolls and peaches with part of mixture.
5 Bake, uncovered, in moderate oven (350°), brushing often with remaining marmalade mixture, 40 minutes, or until richly glazed. Serve over hot buttered noodles, if you wish.

Ham- or Tongue-and-Potato Scallop

All lovers of scalloped potatoes will relish the addition of ham or tongue to their favorite meal

Bake at 350° for 15 minutes.
Makes 6 to 8 servings

6 medium-size potatoes
¼ cup chopped green onions
2 tablespoons butter or margarine
2 tablespoons all-purpose flour
1½ teaspoons salt
¼ teaspoon pepper

1 cup milk
½ cup mayonnaise or salad dressing
4 teaspoons prepared mustard
1 teaspoon Worcestershire sauce
1 pound fresh peas, shelled (1 cup)
6 to 8 slices cooked ham or tongue
1 tablespoon white corn syrup

1 Cook potatoes in boiling salted water in a large saucepan 45 minutes, or until tender; drain. Cool until easy to handle, then peel and slice; place in a large bowl; add green onions.
2 While potatoes cook, melt butter or margarine in a small saucepan; stir in flour, salt and pepper; cook, stirring constantly, just until bubbly.
3 Stir in milk; continue cooking and stirring until sauce thickens and boils 1 minute; remove from heat. Stir in mayonnaise or salad dressing, 3 teaspoons of the mustard and Worcestershire sauce. (Set remaining 1 teaspoon mustard aside for Step 7.)
4 Pour hot sauce over potatoes and onions; toss lightly until potatoes are coated. Spoon onto a large ovenproof platter or into an 8-cup baking dish.
5 Cook peas in boiling salted water in a small saucepan 5 minutes; drain.
6 Overlap tongue or ham slices in a ring on top of potatoes; spoon peas into center.
7 Mix corn syrup and remaining mustard in a cup; brush over tongue or ham.
8 Bake in moderate oven (350°) 15 minutes, or until potatoes are hot and tongue or ham is lightly glazed. Garnish with strips of pimiento, if you wish.

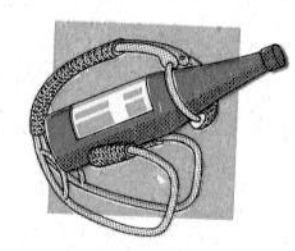

CASSEROLE PASTA KNOW-HOW

Pastas play an important role in many casseroles. Here is a list of some of the most popular:

Pastina—*Tiny pasta bits good for use in soups or as baby food.*
Spaghetti—*The long, round, thin favorite perfect with many kinds of sauces.*
Spaghettini—*A thinner version of spaghetti most preferred in Italy.*
Ziti—*Thicker hollow tubes of pasta that can be served in baked dishes.*
Elbow Macaroni—*Curved hollow tubes most widely used in cold salads, casseroles and macaroni and cheese combinations.*
Fettuccine—*The Romans call it Tagliatelle. Excellent with clam sauce or just butter and grated cheese.*
Linguine—*Long flattened macaroni served with cheese, clam or pesto sauces and grated Parmesan.*
Alphabets—*Letters made of pasta used mainly in soups.*
Lasagna—*Flat, wide ribbons of pasta that come plain, or with a ruffled edge, in white or spinach-flavored green.*
Macaroni Wheels—*Pasta shaped like tiny wagon wheels, used in soups and casseroles, and a favorite with children.*
Ravioli—*Pillow-shaped pasta filled with either meat or cheese. They are first boiled, then combined with a tomato or cheese sauce.*
Farfalle—*Pasta shaped like small bows, used in soups, casseroles, or served alone with sauce.*
Shells—*This pasta comes in small, medium and large sizes. The small ones can be sauced, the larger ones can be stuffed with meat or cheese and baked.*
Manicotti—*Large pasta tubes, first filled with meat or cheese, then baked in a tomato sauce.*
Cannelloni—*Fat, ridged tubes of pasta also suitable for stuffing.*
Vermicelli—*Called 'angel hair' for its fine delicate texture, this spaghetti is best when served with a clam sauce.*
Rigati—*Tubes of pasta more finely ridged than Cannelloni, usually stuffed and baked in tomato sauce.*
Tortellini—*These small pasta rings are filled with meat and dished up in clear consommé, or with a creamy cheese sauce, and topped with Parmesan.*
Noodles—*Flat strands of pasta rich in eggs, and often served as an accompaniment to casserole main dishes such as Beef Stroganoff. Available in plain (white) and spinach (green).*

Eggplant-Ham Bake

Eggplant and ham are baked in layers with sour cream and cheese; add a green salad and dinner is done

Bake at 350° about 30 minutes.
Makes 6 servings

1 medium-size onion, chopped (½ cup)
¼ cup chopped celery
¼ cup chopped green pepper
1 clove of garlic, halved
3 tablespoons butter or margarine
1 cup dairy sour cream
1 teaspoon salt
1 egg, slightly beaten
2 tablespoons milk
⅛ teaspoon pepper
¾ cup fine dry bread crumbs
1 medium-size eggplant, pared and cut into ½-inch slices
12 thin slices cooked ham
¼ pound Muenster or mozzarella cheese, thinly sliced

1 Sauté onion, celery, green pepper and garlic in butter or margarine just until tender; put into small bowl and remove garlic; slowly stir in sour cream and ½ teaspoon salt.
2 Combine egg, milk, ½ teaspoon salt and pepper in shallow dish; place bread crumbs in second dish.
3 Dip eggplant in egg mixture, then in crumbs; brown in a little hot fat, about 3 minutes on each side.
4 Line bottom of shallow oval baking dish, 12x7x2, with eggplant slices; cut 6 large slices in half; stand up around inside of dish.
5 Spread half of sour-cream mixture over eggplant in bottom of dish; top with 6 ham slices and half of the cheese; repeat layers; cover pan with foil.
6 Bake in moderate oven (350°) about 25 minutes, or until bubbly; uncover; bake 5 minutes to brown.

Ham-and-Broccoli Royale

Ham, rice, and broccoli are baked in a cream sauce in this dish fit for a king

Bake at 350° for 45 minutes.
Makes 8 servings

1 cup uncooked regular rice
2 packages (10 ounces each) frozen broccoli spears
6 tablespoons (¾ stick) butter or margarine
2 cups fresh bread crumbs (4 slices)
2 large onions, chopped fine (2 cups)
3 tablespoons all-purpose flour
1 teaspoon salt
¼ teaspoon pepper
3 cups milk
4 cups cubed cooked ham (1½ pounds)
1 package (8 ounces) sliced process white American cheese

1 Cook rice, following label directions; spoon into a greased refrigerator-to-oven baking dish, 13x9x2.
2 Cook broccoli, following label directions; drain well. Place in a single layer over the rice in baking dish.
3 Melt butter or margarine in a large frying pan; measure out 2 tablespoonfuls and sprinkle over bread crumbs in a small bowl; set aside.
4 Stir onions into remaining butter in frying pan; sauté until soft. Stir in flour, salt and pepper; cook, stirring constantly, until bubbly. Stir in milk; continue cooking and stirring until sauce thickens and boils 1 minute. Stir in ham; heat again just until bubbly; pour over layers in baking dish.
5 Place cheese slices over sauce; sprinkle buttered bread crumbs over all. Cover; chill.
6 About 45 minutes before serving time, uncover baking dish; place in moderate oven (350°).
7 Bake 45 minutes, or until bubbly and crumb topping is golden.

Arroz con Cerdo

Toast rice first in frying pan so it will pop open feathery-light when baked with the pork in a saffron-seasoned sauce

Bake at 350° for 1 hour.
Makes 8 servings

8 slices bacon
2 pounds boneless lean pork shoulder, cubed
1 large onion, chopped (1 cup)
1 clove garlic, minced
2 cups uncooked regular rice
5 envelopes instant chicken broth OR: 5 chicken-bouillon cubes
¼ teaspoon crushed saffron
6 cups water
1 pound fresh peas, shelled, cooked, drained, and buttered (1 cup)

Rice and pork combine in **Arroz con Cerdo,** a dish that looks as well on the family table as it does on a buffet.

OR: 1 package (10 ounces) frozen peas, cooked, drained, and buttered
¼ cup chopped peanuts
1 pimiento, diced

1 Sauté bacon until almost crisp in a large frying pan; roll each slice while still warm around tines of a fork to make bacon curls; drain on paper toweling. Set aside for Step 5.
2 Pour all drippings into a cup. Brown pork slowly, a little at a time, in same frying pan; remove.
3 Return 2 tablespoons bacon drippings to pan; add onion and garlic; sauté until soft; push to one side. Add rice and sauté, stirring constantly, until golden. Stir in instant chicken broth or bouillon cubes, saffron, and water; heat to boiling. (If using bouillon cubes, crush with spoon until they are dissolved.)
4 Pour into a 12-cup baking dish; top with browned pork; cover.
5 Bake in moderate oven (350°) 1 hour, or until liquid is absorbed and rice is tender; fluff up with a fork. Stand bacon curls in a ring in center; spoon cooked peas around edge. Sprinkle chopped peanuts and diced pimiento over top.
Note—Saffron, a typical Spanish seasoner, is expensive, but a very little goes a long way to give rice a rich golden color and unusual flavor.

Ham-and-Lima Bake

An old-fashioned dish for budget-wise cooks

Makes 6 servings.

1 pound (2 cups) large dried lima beans
4 cups water
2 teaspoons salt
1 cup grated raw carrots
4 slices bacon
2 cups cubed cooked ham
2 tablespoons vegetable oil
1 large onion, chopped (1 cup)
1 clove of garlic, minced
1 can (about 1 pound) tomatoes
¼ cup molasses

1 Cover lima beans with water in large kettle; heat to boiling; cover; cook 2 minutes. Remove from heat; let stand 30 minutes.
2 Reheat beans to boiling; add salt, grated carrot and bacon. (Do not cut slices.) Cover; cook 45 minutes, or until skins of beans burst when you blow on a few in a spoon.
3 While beans cook, brown ham lightly in vegetable oil in large frying pan. Push to one side of pan and sauté onion and garlic lightly; stir in tomatoes and molasses; cover; simmer 15 minutes.
4 Remove bacon from beans and save for next step. Stir ham mixture into beans; pour into a 12-cup baking dish; cover tightly.
5 Bake in slow oven (325°) 2 hours; remove cover; crisscross saved strips of bacon on top of casserole. Bake 1 hour longer, or until beans are tender.

Linguine alla Maria Teresa

A pasta and ham dish, as elegant as its name; the very thing for a buffet

Bake at 400° for 20 minutes.
Makes 8 servings

1 pound linguine or spaghetti
4 cups diced cooked ham
OR: 1 can (1 pound) ham, diced
6 tablespoons (¾ stick) butter or margarine
1 can (3 or 4 ounces) sliced or chopped mushrooms
4 tablespoons all-purpose flour
1 teaspoon salt
1 tall can (14½ ounces) evaporated milk
1 envelope instant chicken broth
OR: 1 teaspoon granulated chicken bouillon
1⅓ cups water
½ cup grated Romano cheese
1 sweet red pepper
1 green pepper
1 tablespoon butter or margarine (for peppers)
1 cup packaged croutons

1 Cook linguine in a kettle, following label directions; drain; return to kettle.
2 While linguine cooks, brown ham slightly in the 6 tablespoons butter or margarine in a large saucepan; remove with slotted spoon to a small bowl.
3 Drain mushroom liquid into a cup; reserve mushrooms for Step 4. Blend flour and salt into drippings in saucepan; cook, stirring constantly, just until bubbly. Stir in mushroom liquid, milk, chicken broth and water. Continue cooking and stirring until sauce thickens and bubbles 1 minute.
4 Add 2 cups of the sauce and reserved mushrooms to drained linguine; toss to mix. Spoon into a shallow 10-cup baking dish, pressing linguine up sides of dish to leave a hollow in center. Add reserved ham to remaining sauce, blending well. Spoon into hollow in pasta. Sprinkle with Romano cheese.
5 Bake in hot oven (400°) 20 minutes, or until bubbly.
6 Meanwhile, halve, seed and slice peppers; sauté in the 1 tablespoon butter or margarine until soft in a small skillet; keep warm.
7 Sprinkle croutons around edge of casserole and mound sautéed peppers in the center.

Island Pork Pie

Dress up left-over pork roast with bean sprouts and water chestnuts for an Oriental taste treat

Bake at 400° for 30 minutes.
Makes 6 servings

1 medium-size onion, chopped (½ cup)
½ large green pepper, seeded and diced (½ cup)
½ cup thinly sliced celery
1 clove of garlic, minced
2 tablespoons butter or margarine
1 can (10½ ounces) chicken gravy
⅓ cup water
2 tablespoons soy sauce
½ teaspoon salt
Dash of pepper
3 cups diced roast pork
1 can (1 pound) bean sprouts, drained
1 can (5 ounces) water chestnuts, drained and sliced
1 nine-inch frozen pastry shell, thawed

1 Sauté onion, green pepper, celery and garlic in butter or margarine until soft in a large frying pan.
2 Stir in gravy, water, soy sauce, salt, pepper, pork, bean sprouts and water chestnuts; heat to boiling. Spoon into a deep 6-cup baking dish.
3 Spread pastry shell flat, then roll out, if needed, to a round 1 inch larger than baking dish; cut several slits in center to let steam escape. Place over meat filling; fold overhang under, flush with rim; flute edge.
4 Bake in hot oven (400°) 30 minutes, or until pastry is golden.

Confetti Pork Bake

Layers of fluffy rice and lean pork bake in a creamy soup sauce

Bake at 350° about 40 minutes.
Makes 4 servings

¾ cup uncooked regular rice
1 package (10 ounces) frozen green peas
½ cup chopped celery
3 tablespoons butter or margarine
1 cup soft bread crumbs (2 slices)
1 medium-size onion, chopped (½ cup)
3 cups diced roast pork
½ teaspoon leaf marjoram, crumbled
1 can (10¾ ounces) condensed cream of mushroom soup

¾ cup milk
1 pimiento, diced
1 tablespoon chopped parsley

1 Cook rice, following label directions, adding peas and celery during last 5 minutes' cooking.
2 Melt 1 tablespoon butter or margarine in medium-size frying pan; remove from heat; stir in bread crumbs; spoon into a cup and set aside for Step 5.
3 Sauté onion in remaining 2 tablespoons butter or margarine until softened in same frying pan; add pork and brown lightly. Stir in marjoram, mushroom soup and milk until well mixed.
4 Layer rice and meat mixtures into greased 8-cup casserole; top with saved buttered crumbs.
5 Bake in moderate oven (350°) 40 minutes, or until bubbly-hot. Sprinkle pimiento and parsley on top.

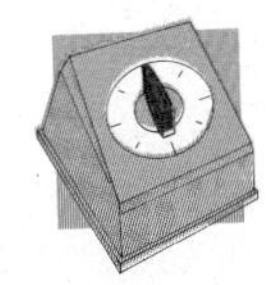

Ham Soufflé

Here's a way to stretch a small amount of ham and save a food budget

Bake at 350° for 45 minutes.
Makes 6 servings

¼ cup (½ stick) butter or margarine
¼ cup sifted all-purpose flour
½ teaspoon dry mustard
¼ teaspoon salt
1 cup milk
¼ cup grated Parmesan cheese
1 cup ground cooked ham
6 eggs, separated

1 Melt butter or margarine in a medium-size saucepan; stir in flour, mustard and salt; cook, stirring constantly, just until bubbly. Stir in milk; continue cooking and stirring until sauce thickens and bubbles 1 minute.
2 Stir in cheese and ham; let cool while beating eggs.
3 Beat egg whites just until they form soft peaks in a large bowl. Beat egg yolks until creamy-thick in a second large bowl; blend in cooled sauce. Stir in about 1 cup of the beaten egg whites until blended, then fold in remainder until no streaks of white remain. Pour into an ungreased 8-cup soufflé or straight-side baking dish. Gently cut a deep circle in mixture about 1 inch from edge with a rubber spatula. (This gives soufflé its double-puff top.)
4 Bake in moderate oven (350°) 45 minutes, or until puffy-firm and golden on top. Serve at once.

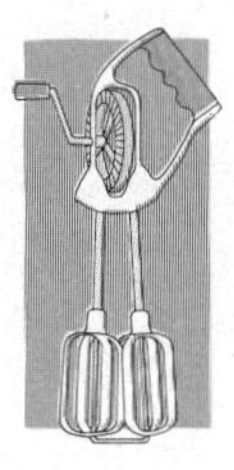

Ham-and-Cheese Soufflé

Swiss cheese and ground ham make this delicately seasoned fancy

Bake at 350° for 45 minutes.
Makes 6 servings

3 tablespoons butter or margarine
3 tablespoons all-purpose flour
½ teaspoon dry mustard
¼ teaspoon salt
1 cup milk
1 cup shredded Swiss cheese (4 ounces)
½ teaspoon caraway seeds
1 cup ground baked ham
6 eggs, separated

1 Melt butter or margarine in a medium-size saucepan; stir in flour, mustard and salt; cook, stirring constantly, just until bubbly. Stir in milk; continue cooking and stirring until sauce thickens and boils 1 minute.
2 Stir in cheese until melted, caraway seeds and ham; let cool while beating eggs
3 Beat egg whites just until they form soft peaks in a large bowl. Beat egg yolks until creamy-thick in a second large bowl; blend in cooled cheese sauce. Stir in about 1 cup of the beaten egg whites until blended, then fold in remaining until no streaks of white remain. Pour into an ungreased 8-cup soufflé or straight-side baking dish. Gently cut a deep circle in mixture about 1 inch in from edge with a rubber spatula. (This gives soufflé its double-puffed top.)
4 Bake in moderate oven (350°) 45 minutes, or until puffy-firm and golden on top. Serve at once.

Curried Ham Soufflé

Here's an ideal way to use bits and pieces of cooked ham, as meat should be ground well

Bake at 350° for 1½ hours.
Makes 6 servings

4 tablespoons (½ stick) butter or margarine
1 small onion, grated
4 tablespoons all-purpose flour
½ teaspoon curry powder
¼ teaspoon salt
Dash of pepper
2 cups milk
½ cup soft bread crumbs (1 slice)
2 cups ground cooked ham (about 1 pound)
4 eggs

1 Melt butter or margarine in a large saucepan. Blend in onion, flour, curry powder, salt and pepper; cook, stirring all the time, just until mixture bubbles.
2 Stir in milk; continue cooking and stirring until sauce thickens and boils 1 minute. Beat in bread crumbs until well blended; remove from heat; stir in ham.
3 Separate eggs, putting whites in a large bowl, yolks in a small bowl. Beat yolks slightly with a fork; blend in a few spoonfuls of the hot ham mixture, then quickly stir back into mixture in saucepan, blending well. Cool to lukewarm.
4 Beat egg whites until they form soft peaks; pour ham mixture over and gently fold in until no streaks of white remain.
5 Spoon into an ungreased 6-cup straight-side baking dish. Set dish in a shallow baking pan; place on oven shelf; pour boiling water into pan to a depth of 1 inch.
6 Bake in moderate oven (350°) 1½ hours, or until soufflé is puffy-light and firm in center. Serve at once.

Sherried Ham Tetrazzini

Three cups of ham cubes with creamy mushroom sauce make this popular main dish

Bake at 400° for 20 minutes.
Makes 6 servings

½ pound thin spaghetti
1 can (3 or 4 ounces) sliced mushrooms
1 medium-size onion, chopped (½ cup)
½ cup chopped celery
6 tablespoons (¾ stick) butter or margarine
6 tablespoons all-purpose flour
2 envelopes instant chicken broth
OR: 2 chicken-bouillon cubes
¼ teaspoon pepper
1 cup cream
3 tablespoons dry sherry
3 cups cubed cooked ham
¼ cup grated Parmesan cheese

1 Break spaghetti in 2-inch pieces. Cook, following label directions; drain; place in a greased shallow 8-cup baking dish.
2 While spaghetti cooks, drain liquid from mushrooms into a 2-cup measure; add water to make 2 cups.
3 Sauté onion and celery in butter or margarine until soft in a large saucepan. Stir in flour, chicken broth or bouillon cubes and pepper. Cook, stirring constantly, until bubbly. Stir in the 2 cups liquid, cream and sherry. Continue cooking and stirring until sauce thickens and boils 1 minute; stir in mushrooms and ham.
4 Spoon over spaghetti in baking dish. Sprinkle with Parmesan cheese.
5 Bake in hot oven (400°) 20 minutes, or until bubbly.

Stuffed Ham Malaga

Slices of meat are folded over rice salad, then glazed with spicy orange sauce

Bake at 350° for 30 minutes.
Makes 6 servings

1 can (about 11 ounces) mandarin-orange segments
¼ cup orange marmalade
¼ teaspoon ground ginger
3 cups cooked rice
¼ cup chopped pecans
3 tablespoons sliced green onion
¼ cup mayonnaise or salad dressing
6 large thin slices baked ham

1 Drain liquid from mandarin-orange segments into a small saucepan; cook rapidly until reduced by half; stir in marmalade and ginger.
2 Set aside 12 mandarin-orange segments; mix remaining with remaining ingredients, except ham, in a bowl. Spoon about ⅔ cup onto each slice of ham; fold ham over to cover filling; place in a shallow baking dish, 10x6x2. Brush with part of the hot orange sauce.
3 Bake in moderate oven (350°), brushing with remaining orange sauce, 25 minutes; garnish with saved mandarin-orange segments; bake 5 minutes longer, or until hot.

Ham Divan

Sliced meat teams with broccoli and a tangy sauce for this second-day best

Bake at 400° for 15 minutes.
Makes 4 servings

1 package (10 ounces) frozen broccoli spears
4 slices white or French bread, toasted and buttered
4 large thin slices baked ham
1 cup (8-ounce carton) dairy sour cream
1 teaspoon prepared mustard
½ cup grated Cheddar cheese

1 Cook broccoli, following label directions; drain well.
2 Place toast slices in a single layer in a large shallow baking dish or in individual baking dishes; cover each with a slice of ham, folding ham, if needed, to fit toast; top with hot broccoli.
3 Blend sour cream with mustard in a small bowl; spoon in ribbons over broccoli; sprinkle with grated cheese.
4 Bake in hot oven (400°) 15 minutes, or until heated through and cheese melts.

LAMB

Lamb Shanks Provencale

Inexpensive lamb shanks and mealy beans combine in a bubbly dinner casserole

Bake at 350° for 2 hours.
Makes 6 servings

1 package (1 pound) dried lima beans or Great Northern white beans
8 cups water
3 medium-size onions, chopped (1½ cups)
2 tablespoons vegetable oil
1 can (1 pound) tomatoes
3 teaspoons salt
1 teaspoon leaf savory, crumbled
2 cloves of garlic, slivered
6 lamb shanks (3½ to 4 pounds)
½ cup water

1 Combine beans with water in a kettle; heat to boiling; boil 2 minutes; cover. Remove from heat; let stand 1 hour.
2 Heat beans to boiling again; reduce heat; cover. Simmer 1½ hours, or until tender. Drain, reserving liquid. Place beans in a large shallow baking dish.
3 Sauté onion in oil until golden, about 8 minutes, in a large skillet. Add to beans; stir in tomatoes, salt and savory.
4 Insert garlic slivers in lamb shanks. Brown shanks on all sides, in same skillet; arrange on top of beans. Pour off all fat from skillet; add water; heat, stirring constantly to loosen browned bits; add to beans. Add enough of reserved liquid to come just to top of beans.
5 Bake, uncovered, in moderate oven (350°) 2 hours, or until meat is tender, stirring occasionally with fork. Add more liquid if needed. Garnish with parsley, if you wish.

Spicy Lamb Casserole

A combination of herbs and spices gives a generous flavor to this dish

2 pounds lean boneless lamb
3 tablespoons butter or margarine
1 large onion, sliced
2 cloves of garlic, minced
2 tablespoons flour
1½ cups water
2 envelopes instant beef broth
½ teaspoon ground cinnamon
½ teaspoon ground ginger
½ teaspoon ground cardamom
⅔ cup golden raisins
1 teaspoon salt
⅛ teaspoon pepper
3 small yellow squashes, cubed
¼ cup lemon juice

1 Cut meat into 2-inch strips. Sauté in butter or margarine until brown in a large skillet; transfer to a 10-cup baking dish.
2 Sauté the onion and garlic in the remaining fat until soft. Stir in the flour, water, beef broth, cinnamon, ginger, cardamom, raisins, salt and pepper. Cook, stirring constantly, 2 minutes.
3 Pour the sauce over the meat. Simmer, covered, for 35 minutes, or until meat is almost tender. Add the squash and lemon juice; continue cooking until squash is tender, about 15 minutes.

Potato Moussaka

Inspired by the classic Greek dish, herbed lamb is here layered with potatoes and baked to make a hearty dish for a brisk day

Makes 6 servings

3 medium-size onions, chopped (1½ cups)
6 tablespoons (¾ stick) butter or margarine
1 pound ground lamb
2 tablespoons minced parsley
½ teaspoon ground thyme
2 teaspoons salt
⅛ teaspoon freshly ground pepper
2 tablespoons flour
¼ cup water
3 eggs
1 cup light cream or milk
2 pounds potatoes, sliced
¼ cup fine dry bread crumbs

1 Sauté the onions in 2 tablespoons of the butter or margarine until soft in a large skillet. Add the meat; cook, stirring constantly, 3 minutes longer. Stir in parsley, thyme, salt, pepper and 1 tablespoon of the flour. Add the water. Cook, stirring constantly, for 2 minutes, or until thickened. Remove from heat; cool.
2 Separate 2 of the eggs; beat yolks with 2 tablespoons of the cream or milk in a small bowl. Stir into the meat mixture. Beat the whites of the 2 eggs until stiff in a small bowl; fold into the meat mixture.
3 Heat 3 tablespoons of the butter or margarine in a large skillet. Add the potatoes; cook, covered, stirring several times until half done.
4 Butter a 10-cup baking dish with remaining butter or margarine; sprinkle with bread crumbs. Layer meat and potatoes in baking dish, ending with potatoes. Bake, uncovered, in moderate oven (350°) for 30 minutes.
5 Beat the remaining flour, cream or milk and egg together in a small bowl; pour over top of potatoes. Bake 10 minutes longer.

Picnic Cassoulet

Lamb and white beans bake to flavorful perfection in seasoned tomatoes

Bake at 400° for 1 hour.
Makes 8 generous servings

4 slices bacon, diced
2 pounds boneless lean lamb shoulder, cut in 1-inch cubes
1 large onion, chopped (1 cup)
¼ pound salami, cut in ¼-inch cubes
2 cans (about 1 pound each) white kidney beans
1 can (about 1 pound) stewed tomatoes
1 teaspoon salt
¼ teaspoon pepper
1 bay leaf

1 Sauté bacon until crisp in a large frying pan; remove with a slotted spoon and place in a 10-cup deep baking dish.
2 Brown lamb slowly, about half at a time, in bacon drippings; drain all drippings from pan. Return all meat to pan; cover. Cook slowly 15 minutes. Remove with a slotted spoon and place in baking dish with bacon.
3 Sauté onion until soft in same frying pan; stir in salami and sauté about 2 minutes. Stir in beans and liquid, tomatoes, salt, pepper, and bay leaf; heat to boiling. Stir into meat mixture; cover.
4 Bake in hot oven (400°) 30 minutes; uncover. Bake 30 minutes longer, or until lamb is tender Remove bay leaf.

Gourmet Lamb Pilaf

Two unusual seeds—coriander and cumin—plus lots of chopped fresh parsley, give this homey casserole an exotic flavor lift

Makes 6 servings
Bake at 350° for 1 hour.

1½ pounds lean lamb shoulder, cubed
½ teaspoon crushed coriander seeds
½ teaspoon crushed cumin seeds
⅛ teaspoon pepper
1 large onion, chopped (1 cup)
¾ cup wheat pilaf (from a 12-ounce package)
1 cup diced celery
1½ teaspoons salt
2 cups water
1 cup chopped parsley

1 Brown lamb cubes, a third at a time, in a medium-size frying pan; spoon into a 6-cup baking dish; stir in coriander and cumin seeds and pepper.
2 Sauté onion until golden in drippings in frying pan; stir in wheat pilaf, celery, salt, and water; heat to boiling. Pour over meat mixture; toss lightly to mix; cover.
3 Bake in moderate oven (350°) 1 hour, or until lamb is tender and liquid is absorbed. Just before serving, stir in parsley.

Lamb Ragout, a one-dish meal, that satisfies the tastebuds of every family member.

Lamb Ragout with Apricots

Rosemary unites the unusual ingredients in this tasty, quick-to-make dish

Makes 4 servings

1 pound boneless lamb shoulder, trimmed
2 tablespoons butter or margarine
1 can (17 ounces) Italian plum tomatoes with juice
½ cup dried apricot halves
½ teaspoon rosemary, crumbled
2 tablespoons dry sherry mixed with 1½ teaspoons cornstarch to thicken sauce (optional)

1 Cut meat into 1-inch cubes; pat dry on paper toweling.
2 Heat butter in large skillet. Brown lamb cubes.
3 Stir tomatoes, apricots and rosemary into skillet.
4 Bring to boiling; lower heat; simmer, covered, for 45 minutes. If too much liquid, uncover last 15 minutes, or thicken with sherry-cornstarch mixture. Taste, add salt and pepper if needed. Serve with kasha or brown rice, and spinach for color contrast.

Lamb-Eggplant Ramekins

Make these exotic little casseroles with layers of seasoned meat and eggplant. A creamy custard topping bakes over all

Bake at 350° for 1 hour and 10 minutes.
Makes 8 servings

1 medium-size eggplant, pared and cut in ¼-inch-thick slices
½ cup olive oil or vegetable oil
4 medium-size onions, sliced
1 clove of garlic, minced
½ pound ground lamb patties
½ pound ground beef
1 can (8 ounces) tomato sauce
1½ teaspoons salt
1 teaspoon leaf oregano, crumbled
2 tablespoons butter or margarine
2 tablespoons all-purpose flour
⅛ teaspoon ground nutmeg
1½ cups milk
½ cup bread crumbs (1 slice)
2 eggs, separated

1 Brown eggplant slices, a few at a time, in olive oil or vegetable oil in a medium-size frying pan,

(continued)

adding oil as needed. Drain well between layers of paper toweling; set aside for Step 6.
2 Sauté onions and garlic just until soft in same pan, adding more oil if needed. Stir in lamb patties and ground beef, breaking up meats with a fork, then stir in tomato sauce, 1 teaspoon salt, and oregano; cover. (Save remaining ½ teaspoon salt for Step 4.)
3 Simmer 30 minutes; remove from heat; let cool while making topping.
4 Melt butter or margarine over low heat in a small saucepan. Stir in flour, saved ½ teaspoon salt, and nutmeg; cook, stirring all the time, just until mixture bubbles. Stir in milk slowly; continue cooking and stirring until sauce thickens and boils 1 minute.
5 Stir bread crumbs and unbeaten egg whites into *cooled* meat mixture. Beat egg yolks slightly in a small bowl; stir in a generous ½ cup of hot sauce; quickly stir back into mixture in saucepan. Cook, stirring constantly, over medium heat 3 minutes, or until thick.
6 Make 2 layers each of eggplant slices and meat mixture in each of 8 greased individual baking dishes; pour sauce over tops. Cover and chill.
7 One hour and 10 minutes before serving time, uncover casseroles; place in a cold oven; set heat control at moderate (350°). Bake 1 hour and 10 minutes, or until custard topping is a rich golden-brown. Garnish each with a green-pepper ring and ripe olives.

Lamb-and-Barley Bake

Two Middle East foods, lamb and barley, are combined with herbs and tomatoes in this savory casserole

Bake at 400° for 45 minutes.
Makes 8 servings

1 cup medium barley
1 envelope (2 to a package) beef flavor mushroom mix
5 cups water
2 pounds ground-lamb patties
2 eggs, beaten
2 tablespoons all-purpose flour
1 teaspoon salt
1 teaspoon mixed salad herbs
2 tablespoons butter or margarine
1 large onion, chopped (1 cup)
1 can (1 pound) stewed tomatoes
¼ cup chopped parsley

1 Combine barley, mushroom mix and water in a large saucepan; heat to boiling; cover. Simmer, stirring several times, 30 minutes, or until barley is tender and almost all liquid is absorbed. Spoon into a 12-cup baking dish.
2 Break up lamb patties and combine with eggs, flour, salt and salad herbs in a large bowl; mix lightly until well blended. Shape into 24 small balls.
3 Brown in butter or margarine in a large frying pan; remove with a slotted spoon and place in baking dish. Pour all drippings from pan, then measure 2 tablespoonfuls and return to pan.
4 Stir in onion; sauté until soft. Stir in tomatoes; heat to boiling. Pour over meat mixture; stir lightly to mix. Do not cover.
5 Bake in hot oven (400°) 45 minutes, or until bubbly. Sprinkle with parsley.

Campground Cassoulet

Lamb and Italian sausage in tandem give an unusual flavor to this stick-to-the-ribs dish

Bake at 400° for 1 hour.
Makes 8 generous servings

4 slices bacon, diced
2 pounds lean boneless lamb shoulder, cut into 1-inch cubes
1 large onion, chopped (1 cup)
1 sweet Italian sausage, sliced ¼-inch thick
2 cans (about 1 pound each) white kidney beans
1 can (about 1 pound) stewed tomatoes
1 teaspoon salt
¼ teaspoon pepper
1 bay leaf

1 Cook bacon until crisp in a large frying pan; remove and place in a 10-cup flameproof bean pot or deep baking dish.
2 Brown lamb slowly, about half at a time, in bacon drippings; drain off all fat. Return all meat to pan; cover. Cook slowly 15 minutes. Remove with slotted spoon and place in bean pot with bacon.
3 Sauté onion just until soft in same frying pan; stir in sausage and sauté about 5 minutes. Add beans and liquid, tomatoes, salt, pepper and bay leaf; heat to boiling. Stir into meat mixture.
4 Bake, covered, in hot oven (400°) 30 minutes; uncover. Bake 30 minutes longer, or until lamb is tender. Remove bay leaf.

What to do with leftovers is often a problem. Here, leftover lamb teams up with eggplant and tomatoes for **Lamb Parmigiana.**

Lamb Parmigiana

Plan to have enough lamb left from a roast to make this bonus treat

Bake at 350° for 1 hour.
Makes 6 servings

4 tablespoons olive oil
1 large eggplant, pared and cut into ½-inch-thick slices
2 tablespoons water
1 large onion, chopped (1 cup)
1 clove garlic, minced
1 can (about 2 pounds) Italian tomatoes
1 tablespoon sugar
2 teaspoons salt
1 teaspoon mixed Italian herbs
¼ teaspoon pepper
4 tablespoons fine dry bread crumbs
3 cups cubed cooked lamb (about 1 pound)
1 package (8 ounces) sliced mozzarella or pizza cheese, cut into strips

1 Spoon 2 tablespoons olive oil into a large frying pan; arrange eggplant slices, slightly overlapping, in pan; drizzle remaining 2 tablespoons olive oil and water over. Cover; steam 15 minutes. Remove eggplant from pan and drain on paper toweling while making sauce.
2 Sauté onion and garlic until soft in same frying pan; stir in tomatoes, sugar, salt, Italian herbs and pepper, then simmer 5 minutes.
3 Arrange half of the eggplant slices in a 10-cup baking dish; sprinkle with 2 tablespoons bread crumbs. Top with half of the lamb and tomato sauce. Repeat with remaining eggplant, bread crumbs, meat and sauce.
4 Bake in moderate oven (350°) 45 minutes, or until mixture starts to bubble in center; crisscross cheese strips on top. Bake 15 minutes longer, or until cheese melts and is creamy-golden.

CREATE YOUR OWN CASSEROLES

Don't sit home worrying about putting a casserole together. Listed here are 130 separate casseroles. Simply take any combination within the charts and you have a casserole that is nutritionally well-balanced.

Here's how they work. Listed are five canned soups, five proteins, five vegetables, and five starches or fillers. You can use the recipe that reads across the chart, or you can take four of the ingredients and substitute an ingredient from the list below. For example, substitute cream of celery soup for golden mushroom soup in the Basic Recipe and the new recipe will read: Cream of celery soup, chicken, spinach and orzo. Do the same for each of the other ingredients, and you have 130 recipes in all.

And so that you can vary your recipes even more, we've split the chart into two sections. You can substitute within each separate chart, or pull from both charts. The second chart contains more highly seasoned combinations.

Combine your four ingredients in a large saucepan; heat just until hot. Turn into a 1½-quart casserole; cover and bake in a moderate oven (350°) for 30 minutes. Add toppings (crushed potato or corn chips, grated cheese, nuts, buttered bread crumbs, chow mein noodles) after baking, if you wish. Makes 4 servings.

CHART I

CONDENSED SOUP	PROTEIN	VEGETABLE	STARCH OR FILLER
Use undiluted		***Thaw frozen vegetables only until they can be mixed in. Or use 1½ cups cooked fresh vegetables.***	***Use 1½ cups, cooked.***
GOLDEN MUSHROOM	Cooked chicken or turkey, cut up (1½ cups). Extra flavor: ⅛ teaspoon tarragon, crumbled	10-ounce package frozen chopped spinach	Orzo (¾ cup uncooked)
SCOTCH BROTH	Cooked lamb, cut up (1½ cups) Extra flavor: ¼ teaspoon rosemary, crumbled	1-pound can tomatoes	Garbanzos or chick peas (1 20-ounce can)
CHEDDAR CHEESE	Tuna (9¼-ounce can, drained). Extra flavor: 2 tablespoons sliced stuffed olives	10-ounce package frozen mixed vegetables	Small pasta shells (¾ cup uncooked)
CREAM OF CELERY	Hard-cooked eggs, cut up (6). Extra flavor: 1 teaspoon curry powder	10-ounce package frozen chopped broccoli	Long-grain rice (½ cup uncooked)
GREEN PEA	Frankfurters, sliced (8 ounces) Extra flavor: ¼ teaspoon oregano, crumbled	9-ounce package frozen Italian green beans	Pinto beans or tomato sauce (1-pound can)

CHART II

CONDENSED SOUP	PROTEIN	VEGETABLE	STARCH OR FILLER
OLD FASHIONED VEGETABLE	Bulk pork sausage (1 pound), browned in skillet. Extra flavor: Top with thin slices of tomato	10-ounce package frozen cut green beans	Hominy (1 pound can)
CHILI BEEF	Cooked ham, cut up (1½ cups). Extra flavor: Top with ½ cup buttered bread crumbs	12-ounce can whole kernel corn with peppers	Elbow macaroni (¾ cup uncooked)
CREAM OF ONION	Cooked beef, cut up (1½ cups). Extra flavor: ¼ teaspoon thyme, crumbled	10-ounce package frozen Danish-style vegetables	Noodles or fettucini (2 cups uncooked)
TOMATO	Ground beef (1 pound), browned with green pepper. Extra flavor: Top with ½ cup shredded cheese	1 cup chopped green pepper, sautéed with beef	Diced potatoes
NEW ENGLAND CLAM CHOWDER	Clams (2 8-ounce cans, undrained). Extra flavor: ¼ teaspoon garlic salt, 2 tablespoons chopped parsley	1-pound can diced carrots, drained	Spaghetti (8 ounces)

POULTRY

Poulet Marengo

Napoleon's chef is said to have created this classic from things at hand; your pantry shelf can supply most of them

Bake at 350° for 1½ hours.
Makes 8 servings

6 slices bacon, cut in 1-inch pieces
2 broiler-fryers (about 2 pounds each), cut up
½ cup sifted all-purpose flour
2 teaspoons salt
¼ teaspoon pepper
2 medium-size onions, chopped (1 cup)
1 clove garlic, minced
1 can (3 or 4 ounces) whole mushrooms
2 cans (1 pound each) tomatoes
¼ cup chopped parsley
Few drops liquid red pepper seasoning
1 cup GOLDEN CROUTONS *(recipe follows)*

1 Fry bacon until almost crisp in large frying pan. Lift out with slotted spoon; drain on paper toweling and set aside for Step 6. Leave drippings in pan.
2 Wash and dry chicken pieces well. Snip off small rib bones with kitchen scissors, if you wish. Shake chicken in mixture of flour, salt, and pepper in paper bag to coat well. (Save any leftover flour mixture for Step 4.)
3 Brown chicken, a few pieces at a time, in bacon drippings; place in 12-cup shallow baking dish.
4 Sauté onion and garlic until soft in same frying pan; stir in saved flour mixture. Drain liquid from mushrooms. (Save mushrooms for Step 6.) Stir liquid, tomatoes, parsley, and liquid red pepper seasoning into frying pan; heat to boiling, stirring constantly.
5 Spoon over chicken in baking dish; cover. (Casserole can be put together up to this point, then chilled. Remove from refrigerator and let stand at room temperature 30 minutes before baking.)
6 Bake in moderate oven (350°) 1 hour and 20 minutes, or until chicken is tender. Uncover; sprinkle with saved bacon pieces and mushrooms. Bake 10 minutes longer, or until bacon is crisp.
7 Just before serving, sprinkle Golden Croutons over top; garnish with more chopped parsley, if you wish.

GOLDEN CROUTONS—Trim crusts from 2 slices of white bread; cut into 1½-inch cubes. Spread in single layer in shallow baking pan. Toast in moderate oven (350°) 10 minutes, or until golden. Makes 1 cup.

Fast Chicken Creole

Popular chicken and rice get a New Orleans accent with canned chicken gumbo soup

Bake at 350° for 30 minutes.
Makes 4 servings

3 cups hot cooked rice
½ cup chopped green pepper
1 medium onion, chopped (½ cup)
½ cup thinly sliced celery
1 clove of garlic, mashed
3 tablespoons butter or margarine
1 can (10¾ ounces) condensed chicken gumbo soup
1 can (1 pound) tomato wedges in tomato juice, drained
1 can (3 or 4 ounces) sliced mushrooms, drained
2 cans (5 ounces each) boned chicken, diced
¼ teaspoon leaf marjoram, crumbled
¼ teaspoon salt
1 package (4 ounces) shredded process American cheese

1 Place cooked rice in a lightly greased 8-cup baking dish.
2 Sauté green pepper, onion, celery, and garlic in butter or margarine until tender in a large saucepan. Stir in remaining ingredients, except cheese. Pour mixture over rice, spreading evenly; sprinkle with cheese; cover.
3 Bake in moderate oven (350°) 30 minutes, or until bubbly-hot.

Chicken Risotto

This quick dish is an excellent and tasty way to use leftover chicken

Bake at 400° for 15 minutes.
Makes 4 servings

1 cup regular uncooked rice
1 cup sliced celery
1 package (10 ounces) frozen green peas
2 cups water (for rice)
2 teaspoons butter or margarine
1 cup diced cooked chicken
2 tablespoons all-purpose flour
⅛ teaspoon pepper
1 small can evaporated milk (⅔ cup)
1⅓ cups water (for sauce)
4 slices process American cheese (4 ounces)
Paprika

1 Combine rice, celery, peas, the 2 cups water, and 1 teaspoon salt in a medium-size saucepan;

(continued)

heat to bubbling; cover; simmer 12 minutes, or until water is absorbed and rice is tender.
2 Melt butter or margarine in a small saucepan; sauté chicken 1 minute; stir in flour, pepper, and remaining 1 teaspoon salt; cook, stirring constantly, just until bubbly. Stir in milk and the 1⅓ cups water; continue cooking and stirring until sauce thickens and boils 1 minute.
3 Pour sauce over rice mixture and toss to combine. Spoon into a buttered shallow 8-cup baking dish. Cut cheese into strips and place in single layer over chicken mixture.
4 Bake in hot oven (400°) for 15 minutes, or until cheese melts and mixture is bubbly-hot. Sprinkle lightly with paprika.

Chicken Napoli

A dish men order when they eat out. Versatile spaghetti-sauce mix does the seasoning

Bake at 350° for 1½ hours.
Makes 6 servings

2 broiler-fryers (about 2 pounds each), cut up
¼ cup sifted all-purpose flour
1 teaspoon salt
⅛ teaspoon pepper
2 tablespoons olive oil or vegetable oil
1 medium-size onion, chopped (½ cup)
1 clove of garlic, minced
1 cup water
1 envelope spaghetti-sauce mix
3 medium-size tomatoes, chopped
¼ cup chopped parsley
6 medium-size potatoes, pared and cut in 1-inch cubes
1 large green pepper, seeded and cut into wide strips

1 Shake chicken with flour, salt, and pepper in paper bag to coat well. Brown, a few pieces at a time, in olive oil or vegetable oil in large frying pan; place in an 8-cup casserole.
2 Sauté onion and garlic until softened in same frying pan; stir in water, then spaghetti-sauce mix; heat to boiling. Stir in tomatoes and parsley. Simmer, uncovered, 15 minutes.
3 Pour over chicken in casserole; top with potato cubes and green pepper strips; cover.
4 Bake in moderate oven (350°) 1½ hours, or until chicken is tender.

Chicken Fiesta

Ready-creamed frozen onions and canned soup make the savory sauce in a hurry

Bake at 350° for 1½ hours.
Makes 8 servings

1 package (8 ounces) medium noodles
1 package (9 ounces) frozen onions in cream sauce
2 cans (10¾ ounces each) condensed golden mushroom soup
1 package (10 ounces) frozen green peas
4 chicken breasts (about 12 ounces each)

1 Cook noodles, following label directions; drain. Combine with onions and 1 can of the mushroom soup in a greased shallow 12-cup baking dish; sprinkle with peas.
2 While noodles cook, pull skin from chicken breasts; cut each in half. Arrange in a single layer over peas; spread with remaining can of soup; cover.
3 Bake in moderate oven (350°) 1½ hours, or until chicken is tender and sauce is bubbly. Garnish with chopped pistachio nuts, if you wish.

Mexicali Chicken

This popular meat cooks the oven-easy way in a just-peppery-enough tomato sauce

Bake at 350° for 1½ hours.
Makes 8 servings

2 broiler-fryers, weighing about 3 pounds each,cut up
2 tablespoons butter or margarine
2 tablespoons olive oil or vegetable oil
1 large onion, chopped (1 cup)
1 large sweet green pepper, quartered, seeded, and chopped
1 large sweet red pepper, quartered, seeded, and chopped
3 teaspoons chili powder
¼ cup sifted all-purpose flour
1 can (about 2 pounds) Italian tomatoes
3 teaspoons salt
1 teaspoon sugar
¼ teaspoon pepper

1 Wash chicken pieces and dry. Brown, part at a time, in butter or margarine and olive oil

(continued)

Mexicali Chicken offers company an inviting, exciting, and colorful eating experience. And this casserole cooks unattended, giving you time for a siesta.

or vegetable oil in a large frying pan; remove all from pan and set aside while making the sauce.
2 Stir onion and green and red peppers into drippings in pan; sauté until soft. Stir in chili powder; cook 1 minute longer.
3 Sprinkle flour over top, then blend in; stir in tomatoes, salt, sugar, and pepper. Cook, stirring constantly, until sauce thickens and boils 1 minute.
4 Layer browned chicken, topping each with part of the sauce, into a 12-cup baking dish; cover.
5 Bake in moderate oven (350°) 1 hour; uncover. Bake 30 minutes longer, or until chicken is tender and sauce is thickened slightly. Garnish with rings of red and green pepper, if you wish.

Paella

Chicken, rice, vegetables and seafood bake in chicken and clam broths in this best-loved Spanish dish

Bake at 350° about 1 hour.
Makes 8 to 10 servings

1 frying chicken, cut in serving-size pieces
2 tablespoons all-purpose flour
¼ cup olive oil or vegetable oil
1½ cups regular uncooked rice
1 large onion, chopped (1 cup)
1 clove of garlic, minced
1 small green pepper, chopped
1 pimiento, cut in thin strips
1 pound fresh peas, shelled
4 tomatoes, peeled and sliced
1 bottle (8 ounces) clam juice
1½ cups water
1 chicken-bouillon cube
½ teaspoon salt
¼ teaspoon pepper
⅛ teaspoon leaf marjoram, crumbled
*2 cans (7½ ounces each) minced clams**
1 pound fresh raw shrimps, shelled and deveined

1 Coat chicken pieces with flour; brown in oil in large frying pan; place in 12-cup baking dish.
2 Sauté rice, onion, garlic, green pepper, and pimiento in oil in frying pan, stirring often, 10 minutes, or until rice is golden; spoon over and around chicken in baking dish; top with peas and tomatoes.
3 Heat clam juice, water, bouillon cube, salt, pepper, and marjoram in same frying pan until cube dissolves; pour over mixture in baking dish; cover.
4 Bake in moderate oven (350°) 30 minutes; add clams and liquid, and shrimps; cover; bake 30 minutes longer, or until chicken and rice are tender.
**Note:* If fresh steamer clams are available, buy 12 to 18 and use in place of canned minced clams. To cook: Scrub shells well; place in large saucepan with 1 cup water; cover; heat to boiling; simmer 3 to 5 minutes, or until shells open. Lift out with tongs; save for Step 4. Strain broth through cheesecloth to remove any sand; measure (there should be 1 cup); add to liquid in Step 3. Use clams in shell in place of 2 cans minced clams in Step 4. Place with shrimps on top of PAELLA.

Senegalese Chicken

Mildly spiced with curry, chicken and noodles bake in a custard-type sauce. Crisp apple and coconut add a festive touch

Bake at 325° for 1 hour and 15 minutes.
Makes 8 servings

1 broiler-fryer (about 3 pounds)
1 small onion, sliced
Few celery tops
1½ teaspoons curry powder
2 teaspoons salt
⅛ teaspoon pepper
1½ cups water
Milk
1 package (8 ounces) fine noodles
1 package (10 ounces) frozen peas
1 can (5 ounces) toasted slivered almonds
4 eggs
1 cup cream for whipping

1 Combine chicken with onion, celery tops, curry powder, salt, pepper, and water in a large saucepan; cover. Simmer 45 minutes, or until tender.
2 Remove chicken from broth; cool until easy to handle. Strain broth into a 2-cup measure; skim any excess fat, then add milk, if needed, to make 2 cups; set aside for Step 5.
3 Pull skin from chicken and take meat from bones. Cut meat into bite-size pieces.
4 While fixing chicken, cook noodles and peas in separate saucepans, following label directions; drain. Combine with chicken and almonds in a buttered 10-cup baking dish.

5 Beat eggs slightly in a medium-size bowl; stir in the 2 cups chicken broth from Step 2 and cream. Pour over chicken mixture, then stir lightly so liquid seeps to bottom.
6 Bake in slow oven (325°) 1 hour and 15 minutes, or until custard sets. (Cover lightly with foil during last 15 minutes' baking to keep top moist.) Garnish with diced red apple and coconut, if you wish.

HOSTESS NOTE: To make ahead, cover chicken-noodle mixture in baking dish and custard mixture in bowl and chill. About 1¼ hours before serving, combine both, following Step 5; place in a cold oven; set heat control at slow (325°). Bake 1 hour and 15 minutes.

Turkey Ramekins

Favorite gourmet-style sauce dresses big cubes of turkey mixed with colorful green and wax beans

Bake at 350° for 30 minutes.
Makes 6 servings

2 packages (10 ounces each) frozen cut green beans
1 package (10 ounces) frozen wax beans
1 tablespoon finely chopped onion
5 tablespoons butter or margarine
5 tablespoons all-purpose flour
½ teaspoon salt
⅛ teaspoon pepper
1 chicken-bouillon cube
OR: 1 envelope instant chicken broth
2 cups milk
4 tablespoons grated Parmesan cheese
2 cups cubed roast turkey
2 tablespoons cream for whipping

1 Cook green and wax beans in separate medium-size saucepans, following label directions; drain well. Set aside ¼ cup of each for garnishing baking dishes in Step 5.
2 Sauté onion in butter or margarine just until soft in a large saucepan. Stir in flour, salt, and pepper; cook, stirring constantly, just until bubbly; add bouillon cube or chicken broth.
3 Stir in milk; continue cooking and stirring until bouillon cube dissolves and sauce thickens and boils 1 minute. Stir in 2 tablespoons of the cheese. Set remaining 2 tablespoons cheese and ½ cup of the sauce aside for topping in Step 6.
4 Stir beans and turkey into remaining sauce; spoon into 6 individual broilerproof baking dishes, or a broilerproof 8-cup shallow baking dish; cover with aluminum foil.
5 Bake in moderate oven (350°) 30 minutes, or until bubbly-hot; remove from oven. Arrange saved beans, spoke fashion, on top.
6 Beat cream until stiff in a small bowl; fold in remaining ½ cup sauce; spoon into centers of baking dishes, dividing evenly. Sprinkle with remaining 2 tablespoons cheese.
7 Broil, about 4 inches from heat, 3 to 5 minutes, or until sauce puffs up and turns golden. Serve at once while sauce is still puffy.

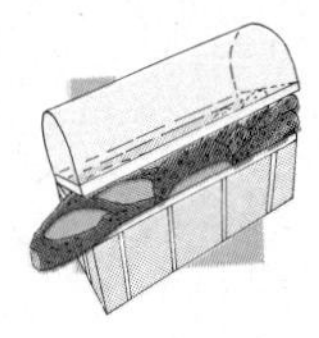

Cassoulet for a Crowd

Turkey, ham, and lima beans are subtly seasoned and baked to provide the star of a buffet

Bake at 350° for 1½ hours.
Makes 12 to 16 servings

1 frozen turkey (about 6 pounds), thawed
2 ham hocks (about 1 pound each)
8 cups water
1 cup grated carrot (2 medium-size)
2 large onions, chopped (2 cups)
3 teaspoons salt
2 cloves of garlic, sliced
2 bay leaves
1 teaspoon leaf thyme, crumbled
3 sprigs of parsley
4 cups dried large lima beans (from a 2-pound bag)

1 Place turkey with giblets and ham hocks in a kettle or Dutch oven. Add water, carrot, onion, and salt.
2 Place garlic, bay leaves, thyme, and parsley sprigs in a piece of cheesecloth and tie with a string. Push under liquid in kettle.
3 Heat slowly to boiling; reduce heat; cover. Simmer 1 hour, or until turkey is tender. Discard herb bag. Place meats, giblets and liquid in one or two large bowls and chill. (Overnight is best.)
4 Remove meats and giblets from liquid; reserve liquid. Take skin, fat, and bones from turkey and ham; cut meats and giblets into small pieces; reserve in refrigerator.
5 Pick over beans; combine with reserved broth in a kettle; heat to boiling and boil 2 minutes; cover. Remove from heat; let stand 1 hour.

(continued)

6 Heat beans to boiling again; reduce heat; cover. Simmer 2 hours, or until beans are tender. Add reserved meats and giblets; toss lightly to mix. Spoon into a 16-cup baking dish or two 8-cup baking dishes.
7 Bake in moderate oven (350°) 1½ hours, or until bubbly in center. Sprinkle with chopped parsley, if you wish.

Turkey Salad Bake

Leftover turkey is the start of this unusual salad; you can do it in about 30 minutes

Bake at 450° for 10 minutes.
Makes 4 servings

2 cups finely crushed potato chips (about a 4-ounce package)
½ cup grated sharp Cheddar cheese
½ cup chopped walnuts
1 tablespoon butter or margarine
2 cups cubed cooked turkey
2 cups thinly sliced celery
2 teaspoons grated onion
¼ teaspoon salt
2 tablespoons lemon juice
½ cup mayonnaise or salad dressing

1 Mix potato chips and cheese in small bowl; pat half of mixture into bottom of a shallow 6-cup baking dish. (Save remaining for topping in Step 3.)
2 Sauté walnuts in butter or margarine in small frying pan, stirring often, 15 minutes, or until lightly toasted; drain on paper toweling. Toss with remaining ingredients in medium-size bowl.
3 Spoon into prepared baking dish; sprinkle saved potato-chip mixture on top.
4 Bake in very hot oven (450°) 10 minutes, or until hot and golden.

Turkey Cassoulet

A popular French casserole inspired this inviting way with turkey

Bake at 350° for 1½ hours.
Makes 6 servings

1 pound (2 cups) large dried lima beans
4 cups water
1 can (about 1 pound) tomatoes
6 slices bacon
1 cup grated raw carrots
1 large onion, chopped (1 cup)
2 teaspoons salt
1 teaspoon leaf thyme, crumbled
1 teaspoon leaf basil, crumbled
1 bay leaf
¼ teaspoon pepper
2 cups diced cooked turkey
1 cup chopped celery
¼ cup whole-fruit cranberry sauce

1 Combine lima beans and water in large kettle. Heat to boiling; cover; cook 2 minutes. Remove from heat; let stand 1 hour.
2 Stir in tomatoes, bacon slices, carrots, onion and seasonings; cover. Heat to boiling; simmer 1 hour, or until skins of beans burst when you blow on a few in a spoon.
3 Lift bacon slices from beans and save for next step; remove bay leaf. Stir turkey, celery and cranberry sauce into beans; pour into 10-cup baking dish; cover.
4 Bake in moderate oven (350°) 1 hour. Uncover; crisscross saved bacon slices on top. Bake 30 minutes longer, or until liquid is absorbed.

Deep Dish Turkey Pie

It's biscuit-topped, with chunks of turkey and vegetables in a savory sauce

Bake at 425° for 30 minutes.
Makes 6 servings

6 medium-size potatoes, pared and quartered
6 medium-size carrots, scraped and quartered
1 small onion, chopped (¼ cup)
¼ cup chopped green pepper
2 tablespoons butter or margarine
1 can (10¾ ounces) condensed cream of chicken soup
3 cups cooked turkey chunks
Biscuit-Wedge Topping (recipe follows)

1 Cook potatoes and carrots in boiling salted water in large saucepan 15 to 20 minutes, or until tender; drain, saving 1 cup of liquid for next step.
2 While vegetables cook, sauté onion and green pepper in butter or margarine until soft in saucepan; stir in chicken soup and 1 cup saved liquid.

3 Spoon vegetables and turkey into 8-cup casserole: pour sauce over.
4 Bake in hot oven (425°) 15 minutes while making *Biscuit-Wedge Topping;* arrange biscuits on top of hot mixture; bake 15 minutes longer, or until biscuits are golden.

BISCUIT-WEDGE TOPPING—Sift 1½ cups sifted all-purpose flour, 2 teaspoons baking powder, and ½ teaspoon salt into medium-size bowl; cut in ¼ cup (½ stick) butter or margarine; add ½ cup milk all at once; stir just until blended. Turn dough out onto lightly floured pastry cloth or board; knead lightly ½ minute; roll out to a 7-inch round; cut into 6 wedges; brush tops lightly with milk; sprinkle with ¼ teaspoon poppy seeds.

Turkey Tetrazzini

Turkey stars in this version of the dish made famous by Madame Tetrazzini

Bake at 350° for 1 hour.
Makes 6 servings

1 package (8 ounces) thin spaghetti
4 tablespoons (½ stick) butter or margarine
4 tablespoons flour
¼ teaspoon salt
2 cups milk
1 can (3 or 4 ounces) sliced mushrooms
2 cups diced cooked turkey
1 can (4 ounces) pimientos, diced
2 tablespoons grated Parmesan cheese

1 Cook spaghetti, following label directions; drain. Place in a buttered 8-cup casserole.
2 While spaghetti cooks, melt butter or margarine over low heat in a medium-size saucepan. Blend in flour and salt; cook, stirring all the time, just until mixture bubbles. Stir in milk slowly, then liquid from mushrooms, plus enough water to make 1 cup; continue cooking and stirring until sauce thickens and boils 1 minute.
3 Stir in mushrooms, turkey, and pimientos; spoon over spaghetti; sprinkle with cheese.
4 Bake uncovered in moderate oven [350°] about 1 hour.

SAUSAGES AND FRANKS

Shepherdess Pie

Soup mix boosts the flavor of this hearty meat-and-potato casserole

Bake at 350° for 45 minutes.
Makes 4 servings

1 package (8 ounces) heat-and-serve sausage patties
2 tablespoons all-purpose flour
2 cups water
1 envelope (2 to a package) vegetable-beef soup mix
4 cups hot mashed potatoes
½ cup crumbled whole-wheat wafers

1 Cut each sausage patty into about 10 small pieces; brown, stirring frequently, in a medium-size skillet. Blend in flour; cook, stirring constantly, just until bubbly. Stir in water and soup mix; continue cooking and stirring until gravy thickens and boils 5 minutes.
2 Line bottom and sides of a buttered deep 6-cup baking dish with 3 cups of the mashed potatoes. Spoon in sausage and gravy; spoon remaining potatoes in mounds over top; sprinkle with crumbled wafers.
3 Bake in moderate oven (350°) 45 minutes, or until bubbly-hot. Sprinkle with finely cut parsley, if you wish.

Beanie Bake

Two big favorites—canned beans and franks—star in this stick-to-the-ribs casserole

Bake at 375° for 35 minutes.
Makes 6 servings

6 tablespoons molasses
2 tablespoons prepared mustard
1 teaspoon instant coffee powder
3 cans (about 1 pound each) baked beans
2 tablespoons cider vinegar
1 pound frankfurters, halved crosswise
½ cup French-fried onion rings (from an about-4-ounce can)

1 Mix molasses, mustard, and instant coffee in a cup.

(continued)

2 Place beans in an 8-cup shallow baking dish; stir in vinegar and all but about 2 tablespoons of the molasses mixture. (Remaining is for brushing franks in next step.)
3 Arrange halved frankfurters in a chevron design on top; brush with remaining molasses mixture. Crush onion rings and sprinkle evenly over the top.
4 Bake in moderate oven (375°) 35 minutes, or until bubbly-hot.

Baked Bologna Jubilee

Buy bologna by the piece, stud it with cloves and bake with fruits for a different and spectacular creation

Bake at 350° for 30 minutes.
Makes 8 servings

1 piece bologna, weighing about 3 pounds
Whole cloves
4 cups mixed sliced or cut-up pared fresh fruits
1 cup firmly packed light brown sugar
¼ teaspoon ground cinnamon
¼ cup orange juice
2 tablespoons lemon juice
2 tablespoons butter or margarine

1 Peel covering, if any, from bologna; cut bologna in half lengthwise. Score rounded side of each half in diamond pattern; stud meat with whole cloves. Place halves, cut sides down, in a greased baking dish, 13x9x2. Arrange fruits around meat.
2 Blend brown sugar, cinnamon, and orange and lemon juices in a small bowl; drizzle over meat and fruits. Dot fruits with butter or margarine; cover pan.
3 Bake in moderate oven (350°) 20 minutes; uncover. Spoon juices in dish over meat. Bake 10 minutes longer, or until lightly glazed.

Baked Bologna Jubilee makes exciting eating because of a unique recipe. Hint when shopping: bologna is available in single pieces as well as slices.

CASSEROLES FOR THE DIET FAN

Because casseroles are packed with one-dish ingredients, often they are high in calories. Seemingly, there is little you can do to cut out some of those bulge-builders.

We have drawn up a short list of ways you can trim the calories from your favorite casseroles without interfering with taste.

- *Trim all visible fat from meat before browning or braising.*
- *Brown meats in a nonstick skillet.*
- *Substitute cooked shredded cabbage, lettuce or spinach for the bed of pasta or rice in your favorite recipe.*
- *Use skim milk, skim evaporated milk or chicken or beef broth for cream and whole milk in sauces.*
- *Substitute low-fat cheese, such as low-fat cottage cheese and low-fat mozzarella, for whole-milk cheese.*
- *Remove every speck of fat from stews or pot roasts before thickening gravy by refrigerating food or adding a few ice cubes to liquid. Wait for fat to harden, then skim off.*

Calico Franks

Frozen mixed vegetables with sauce speed the making of this light main dish.

Bake at 375° for 30 minutes.
Makes 4 servings

2 packages (8 ounces each) frozen mixed vegetables with onion sauce
1½ cups milk
1 pound frankfurters, sliced
1 cup soft bread crumbs (2 slices)
1 package (4 ounces) shredded Cheddar cheese

1 Combine frozen vegetables with milk in a large saucepan; heat, following label directions. Stir in frankfurters; spoon half into a 6-cup baking dish.
2 Mix bread crumbs and cheese in a small bowl; sprinkle half over layer in baking dish. Top with remaining vegetable mixture, then remaining crumb mixture.
3 Bake in moderate oven (375°) 30 minutes, or until casserole is bubbly in center and crumb topping is golden.

Bratwurst Bake

A flavorful tomato sauce adds zest to sausages and chick peas

Bake at 350° for 45 minutes.
Makes 6 servings

6 fully cooked bratwurst
1 tablespoon vegetable oil
1 large onion, peeled and sliced
1 clove of garlic, minced
1 can (1 pound) Italian tomatoes
1 can (6 ounces) tomato paste
1 tablespoon leaf oregano, crumbled
1½ teaspoons salt
¼ teaspoon pepper
1 tablespoon bottled steak sauce
2 cans (1 pound, 4 ounces each) chick peas, drained

1 Brown bratwurst in vegetable oil in a Dutch oven; remove from pan with a slotted spoon.
2 Add onion and garlic to drippings in Dutch oven; sauté until soft.
3 Stir in tomatoes and paste, oregano, salt, pepper, steak sauce and chick peas. Heat 3 minutes, or until bubbly. Arrange bratwurst on top. Do not cover.
4 Bake in moderate oven (350°) 45 minutes, or until bubbly.
Note—Chill if made ahead, then reheat on grill at your eating spot.

A stew is a stew, but not when it is **Calico Veal Fricassee,** a mild-flavored combination of veal, potatoes, and peppers.

Cold Weather Stews

Casseroles that beat the winter blahs are the highlight in this chapter. They are grouped according to the main meat used. And for your further convenience, the number of servings is set apart before the recipe ingredients.

Calico Veal Fricassee

This mild-flavor meat, green and red peppers and speedy canned potatoes blend in a delicately seasoned cream-rich gravy

Makes 8 servings

3 pounds lean boneless veal shoulder
4 tablespoons vegetable oil
1 large onion, chopped (1 cup)
1 clove garlic, crushed
1 cup water
2 envelopes instant chicken broth OR: 2 chicken-bouillon cubes
1½ teaspoons salt
2 cans (1 pound each) small white potatoes, drained and halved
1 small green pepper, halved, seeded and sliced
1 small red pepper, halved, seeded and sliced
¾ cup light cream or table cream

1 Trim any fat from veal; cut veal into 1-inch cubes. Brown, half at a time, in vegetable oil in a kettle or Dutch oven; remove and set aside.
2 Stir onion and garlic into drippings in kettle; sauté just until soft. Return all veal to kettle.
3 Stir in water, chicken broth or bouillon cubes and salt; cover.
4 Simmer 45 minutes; add potatoes and green and red peppers; cover again. Simmer 20 minutes longer, or until veal and peppers are tender.
5 Stir in cream; simmer 10 minutes to blend flavors. Serve over hot cooked noodles, if you wish.

Hawaiian Veal Curry

Spicy-hot and fruity as curry should be—and the flavor becomes mellower upon standing

Makes 4 servings

1½ pounds veal shoulder, cut in 1-inch cubes
2 tablespoons vegetable oil
1 tablespoon curry powder
⅛ teaspoon ground ginger
1 large onion, chopped (1 cup)
1 can dry cream of mushroom soup mix
1 teaspoon salt
⅛ teaspoon pepper
1 can (3 or 4 ounces) sliced mushrooms
1 can (about 14 ounces) pineapple tidbits
1 cup water
Fluffy hot rice

1 Brown veal in vegetable oil in large frying pan; remove and set aside. Blend curry powder and ginger into drippings in pan; add onion and sauté just until soft.
2 Stir in browned meat and remaining ingredients, except rice; heat to boiling; cover.
3 Simmer, stirring often, 1 hour, or until veal is tender.
4 Serve over fluffy hot rice, with your choice of condiments, such as bottled chutney, flaked coconut, sweet-pickle relish, diced banana, crisp bacon bits.

Veal Ragout

Delicate veal is lightly seasoned with rosemary, cooked with potatoes, and served with squash and green beans

Makes 4 servings

1 pound lean veal shoulder, cubed
1 large onion, peeled and sliced thin
2 cups shredded lettuce
1 teaspoon salt
Dash of pepper
½ teaspoon leaf rosemary, crumbled
1 envelope instant chicken broth OR: 1 chicken-bouillon cube
1 cup hot water
8 small new potatoes
2 medium-size yellow squashes
½ pound green beans
2 tablespoons cornstarch
2 tablespoons cold water

1 Trim all fat from veal. Combine veal, onion, lettuce, salt, pepper and rosemary in a kettle or Dutch oven.
2 Dissolve instant chicken broth or bouillon cube in hot water in a 1-cup measure; pour over

(continued)

veal; cover. Simmer 2 hours, or until veal is tender.
3 About 45 minutes before meat is done, scrub potatoes well; cut off a band of skin around middle of each. Wash, trim and slice squashes thin. Wash, tip and cut green beans diagonally into ½-inch-long pieces.
4 Place potatoes on top of meat mixture; cook 30 minutes, or until tender. Cook squashes and green beans in slightly salted boiling water in separate medium-size saucepans 15 minutes, or until crisply tender; drain; keep hot.
5 Smooth cornstarch and cold water to a paste in a cup; stir into hot meat mixture. Cook, stirring constantly, until broth thickens and boils 3 minutes.
6 Spoon meat mixture, dividing evenly, and 2 potatoes into each of 4 heated serving dishes; spoon squash and green beans in separate piles at edge.

Veal Provençale

Basic to the fine flavor of both veal and cream gravy: Beef broth, wine and herbs

Makes 8 servings

3 pounds veal shoulder, cut into 1-inch cubes
¼ cup vegetable oil
1 medium-size onion, chopped (½ cup)
1 clove of garlic, minced
1 envelope instant beef broth
OR: 1 beef-bouillon cube
1 teaspoon paprika
½ teaspoon celery salt
½ teaspoon pepper
½ teaspoon leaf rosemary, crumbled
1 can (6 ounces) sliced mushrooms
1 cup water
⅔ cup sherry
3 tablespoons all-purpose flour
1 cup (8-ounce carton) dairy sour cream

1 Brown veal cubes, a few at a time, in vegetable oil in a large frying pan; remove with a slotted spoon; set aside.
2 Stir onion and garlic into drippings in pan; sauté until soft. Stir in beef broth or bouillon cube, paprika, celery salt, pepper, rosemary, mushrooms and liquid, water and sherry; add veal cubes; heat to boiling.
3 Simmer 1 hour, or until veal is tender; chill.
4 About 15 minutes before serving, heat veal mixture to boiling.
5 Blend flour and a little water to a paste in a cup; stir into veal. Cook, stirring constantly, until gravy thickens and boils 1 minute. Stir about ½ cup of the gravy into sour cream in a small bowl, then stir back into remaining veal mixture in frying pan. Heat very slowly, stirring constantly, *just* until hot. (Do not boil.) Just before serving, garnish with lemon slices, if you wish.

Paprikash Casserole

Veal, noodles, and paprika will bring memories and thoughts of Hungary

Bake at 400° about 1 hour.
Makes 6 servings

2 pouhds veal for stewing, cut into 1-inch cubes
1 tablespoon all-purpose flour
1 tablespoon paprika
1½ teaspoons salt
2 tablespoons vegetable shortening
2 cans (about 1 pound each) tomatoes
1 envelope onion-soup mix
2 teaspoons sugar
⅛ teaspoon pepper
½ pound regular noodles
1 tablespoon butter or margarine
1 cup (8-ounce carton) dairy sour cream
¼ teaspoon caraway seeds

1 Shake veal with flour, paprika and salt in a paper bag to coat well.
2 Brown about half the meat at a time slowly in shortening in large frying pan; return all meat to pan; stir in tomatoes, onion-soup mix, sugar and pepper; cover tightly; simmer, stirring a few times, 30 to 45 minutes, or until meat is tender; pour into a 10-cup ovenproof casserole.
3 While meat simmers, cook noodles in a large saucepan, following label directions; drain; return to saucepan; add butter or margarine; toss to coat well; spoon on top of meat in casserole but do not stir in (noodles keep their color best if not mixed with sauce); cover; chill.
4 About 1 hour before serving time, place casserole in cold oven; set heat control at hot (400°); bake, covered, 1 hour, or until bubbly-hot; uncover; stir in sour cream and caraway seeds; bake just 5 minutes longer (do not overcook, as sour cream may curdle).

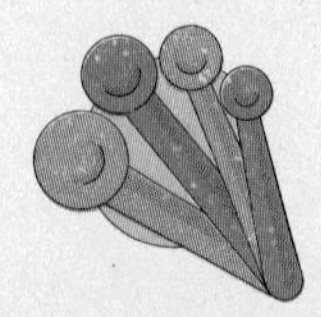

Continental Beef Bounty

Dumplings bake crusty-golden atop meat and vegetables in rich gravy. Italian sausages add a spicy flavor

Bake at 350° for 2½ hours.
Makes 8 servings

1 large Bermuda onion, sliced
2 tablespoons vegetable shortening
2 sweet Italian sausages, sliced
2 pounds lean beef for stewing
3 tablespoons all-purpose flour
1 pound carrots, pared and cut in 2-inch lengths
2 cans (12 ounces each) mixed vegetable juice
1½ teaspoons salt
10 peppercorns
2 bay leaves
1 small head (about 1 pound) cauliflower
GOLDEN DUMPLING PUFFS *(recipe follows*
1 cup sliced celery

1 Sauté onion slices in shortening until soft in a large frying pan; lift out with a slotted spoon and place in a 12-cup baking dish. Brown sausages in drippings in pan; combine with onion.
2 Trim any fat from beef; cut beef into 1-inch cubes. Shake with flour in a paper bag to coat evenly. Brown, half at a time, in same frying pan; add to onion mixture with carrots.
3 Stir vegetable juice and salt into pan; heat to boiling, scraping browned bits from bottom of pan; pour over meat mixture. Tie peppercorns and bay leaves in a tiny cheesecloth bag; add to baking dish; cover.
4 Bake in moderate oven (350°) 1½ hours.
5 While meat cooks, trim cauliflower; break into flowerets. Parboil in boiling water in a medium-size saucepan 5 minutes; drain. Make GOLDEN DUMPLING PUFFS.
6 Stir cauliflower and celery into hot stew mixture; drop dumpling batter in 8 mounds around top.
7 Bake, uncovered, 1 hour longer, or until meat and vegetables are tender and dumplings are puffed and golden. Remove seasoning bag before serving.

GOLDEN DUMPLING PUFFS—Melt 2 tablespoons butter or margarine in a small saucepan; stir in ¼ cup sifted all-purpose flour and ¼ teaspoon salt. Cook, stirring constantly, just until bubbly; stir in ½ cup milk. Continue cooking and beating until mixture forms a thick smooth ball that follows spoon around pan. Remove from heat; cool slightly. Separate 1 egg, placing white in a small bowl; beat yolk into cooled mixture until thick and shiny-smooth. Beat egg white until it stands in firm peaks; fold into yolk mixture until no streaks of white remain.

Beef Jardinière with Marrow Dumplings

Here's French-flair cooking on a shoestring budget

Makes 4 servings

1½ pounds beef chuck, cubed
1 can (about 1 pound) tomatoes
1 cup water
1 teaspoon sugar
1 teaspoon salt
1 bay leaf
½ teaspoon leaf thyme, crumbled
¼ teaspoon pepper
MARROW DUMPLINGS *(recipe follows)*
4 carrots, pared and cut into 3-inch lengths
1 can (about 1 pound) green peas

1 Trim all fat from beef; brown beef quickly in a few melted trimmings in large frying pan; stir in tomatoes, water and seasonings. Cover; simmer 1 hour, or just until meat is tender.
2 While stew cooks, make and shape MARROW DUMPLINGS; chill.
3 Add carrots to hot stew; cook 25 minutes, or until tender. Stir in peas; arrange MARROW DUMPLINGS on top; cover; cook 5 minutes longer.

Marrow Dumplings

If you have never made these, we think you will find them a real treat

Makes about 12 small balls

Beef marrow from a 3- to 4-inch beef marrowbone (½ cup mashed)
1 egg
1 cup soft bread crumbs (2 slices)
1 tablespoon chopped parsley
½ teaspoon salt
⅛ teaspoon pepper

1 Cut out marrow with a sharp thin-blade knife; mash to make ½ cup. Combine with remaining ingredients in small bowl; blend well.
2 Form lightly into marble-size balls. Set in a

(continued)

shallow pan; chill at least 1 hour. (Dumplings will hold their shape better when chilled before cooking.)
3 Cook, covered, on top of hot beef mixture 5 minutes.

Lancashire Hot Pot

Two meats—beef chuck and veal kidney—make this classic meat-and-potato hearty

Bake at 350° for 3 hours.
Makes 6 to 8 servings

1½ pounds beef chuck, cut in 1-inch cubes
2 veal kidneys
¼ cup unsifted all-purpose flour
2 beef-bouillon cubes
2 cups boiling water
1 teaspoon Worcestershire sauce
6 medium-size potatoes, pared and sliced thin (6 cups)
3 large onions, sliced
2 teaspoons salt
¼ teaspoon pepper
2 tablespoons butter or margarine

1 Trim all fat from beef. Halve kidneys; cut out tubes and white membrane, then cut kidneys into ½-inch cubes. Shake meats, a few cubes at a time, with flour in a paper bag to coat well.
2 Dissolve bouillon cubes in boiling water in a 2-cup measure; stir in Worcestershire sauce.
3 Layer vegetables and meats into a 12-cup deep baking dish this way: Half of each of potatoes, onions and meats, sprinkling each layer lightly with salt and pepper. Repeat with remaining vegetables, meats, salt and pepper.
4 Pour bouillon mixture over; dot with butter or margarine; cover.
5 Bake in moderate oven (350°) 3 hours, or until beef is tender.

Beef-Vegetable Ragout

Each man-size serving boasts lots of meat, a whole potato and four vegetables

Makes 6 servings

1 small onion, chopped (¼ cup)
½ cup water (for onion)
1½ pounds lean beef round or chuck, cut into 1-inch cubes
1 bay leaf
½ teaspoon seasoned salt
¼ teaspoon seasoned pepper
1 can (10½ ounces) condensed beef bouillon
1 cup water (for ragout)
6 small potatoes, pared
3 cups sliced celery
1 small eggplant, diced (3 cups)
1 teaspoon sugar
½ small head of escarole, chopped (3 cups)
3 medium-size tomatoes, cut into wedges

1 Simmer onion in ½ cup water in large heavy kettle or Dutch oven 10 minutes, or just until water evaporates. Continue cooking and stirring over low heat until onion browns lightly; remove and set aside.
2 Brown beef cubes, a few at a time, in same kettle. (No need to add fat.) Return all beef and onion to kettle; stir in bay leaf, seasoned salt and pepper, beef bouillon and 1 cup water. Heat to boiling; cover; simmer 1½ to 2 hours, or just until beef is tender.
3 Arrange potatoes on top; cover; simmer 30 minutes. Add celery and eggplant; simmer 10 minutes longer, or until potatoes are tender.
4 Stir in sugar. Lay escarole and tomatoes on top; cover again; simmer 5 minutes, or just until greens are wilted. Remove bay leaf.
5 Spoon a potato in the middle of each heated serving dish; surround with ragout. Garnish with dill-pickle strips, if you wish.

Beef "Burgundy"

A simplified version of a French classic

Bake at 325° for 2 hours.
Makes 6 servings

4 slices bacon, cut in ½-inch pieces
2 pounds lean beef chuck, shank or round, cut in 1-inch cubes
6 small carrots
1 parsnip
1 medium-size onion, chopped (½ cup)
1 cup tomato juice
1 cup red Burgundy wine
1 teaspoon salt
8 peppercorns
4 whole cloves
1 bay leaf
1 beef-bouillon cube
12 small white onions, peeled
1 cup frozen peas (from a 1½-pound bag)

1 Sauté bacon until crisp in a large frying pan; remove and set aside for Step 7. Brown beef cubes, a few at a time, in the bacon drippings, then place in an 8-cup baking dish.
2 Pare carrots and parsnip. Dice 1 carrot and the thin end of parsnip; sauté with onion, stirring often, until golden, in same frying pan. (Set remaining carrots and parsnip aside for Step 5.)
3 Stir in tomato juice, wine, salt, peppercorns, cloves, bay leaf and bouillon cube; heat to boiling, crushing bouillon cube with a spoon until it dissolves. Pour over meat in baking dish; cover.
4 Bake in slow oven (325°) 1 hour.
5 While stew bakes, cut remaining carrots and parsnip into 2-inch-long sticks; add with white onions to stew; cover again.
6 Bake 45 minutes longer, or just until meat and vegetables are tender. Stir in peas; cover and cook 15 minutes longer.
7 Let stew stand 5 to 10 minutes until any fat rises to top, then skim off. Garnish stew with bacon.

Algonquin Beef and Squash Bake

Chunks of chuck are layered with potatoes and onions and topped with acorn squash for a hearty country-style dinner

Bake at 350° for 3 hours.
Makes 6 to 8 servings

2 pounds beef chuck, cut in 1-inch cubes
¼ cup unsifted all-purpose flour
2 cups tomato juice
2 beef-bouillon cubes
1 tablespoon brown sugar
¼ cup finely chopped parsley
2 cloves of garlic, minced
3 teaspoons salt
¼ teaspoon pepper
¼ teaspoon ground nutmeg
4 medium-size potatoes, pared and sliced thin (4 cups)
8 small onions, peeled and quartered
1 acorn squash, split and seeded
2 tablespoons butter or margarine

1 Trim all fat from beef. Shake cubes, a few at a time, with flour in a paper bag to coat well.
2 Combine tomato juice, bouillon cubes and sugar in a small saucepan; heat, crushing cubes to dissolve, just to boiling.
3 Combine parsley, garlic, salt, pepper and nutmeg in a cup.
4 Layer vegetables and meat into a 12-cup deep baking dish this way: Half of each of potatoes, onions and beef, sprinkling each layer lightly with seasoning mixture. Repeat with remaining potatoes, onions, beef and seasoning mixture.
5 Cut each squash half into 6 slices; pare; arrange on top. Pour hot tomato-juice mixture over; dot with butter or margarine; cover.
6 Bake in moderate oven (350°) 3 hours, or until beef is tender.

Baked Oxtail Ragout

Oxtails are moderately priced, and so are budget saving; here they simmer lazily in a hearty sauce

Bake at 375° for 2 hours.
Makes 8 servings

4 pounds oxtails
½ cup unsifted all-purpose flour
1 teaspoon salt
1 teaspoon leaf savory, crumbled
¼ teaspoon pepper
¼ cup vegetable oil
1 large onion, chopped (1 cup)
1 can (12 ounces) carrot juice
1½ cups water
½ cup dry red wine
1 bay leaf

1 Cut oxtails into uniform-length pieces.
2 Shake pieces in a mixture of flour, salt, savory and pepper in a plastic bag to coat well; reserve remaining seasoned flour (you should have about 2 tablespoons).
3 Brown pieces slowly, part at a time, in oil in a large skillet; remove pieces with a slotted spoon to an 8-cup baking dish.
4 Stir onion into drippings in skillet; sauté until soft. Stir in reserved seasoned flour; cook, stirring, just until bubbly. Stir in carrot juice, water and wine; continue cooking and stirring, until gravy thickens and bubbles 1 minute. Pour over meat in baking dish; add bay leaf; cover.
5 Bake in moderate oven (375°) 2 hours, or until meat separates easily from bones.
6 Ladle ragout into soup plates; serve with French bread, if you wish.

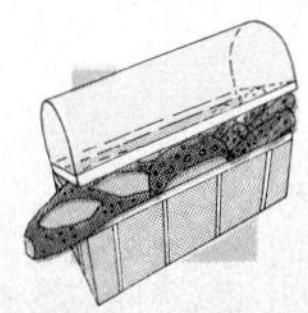

HOW TO MAKE A SAUCE

There is little to making a sauce. Anyone can do it, providing the basics are learned. And once you've got the basics for sauce-making under control, you can use the same techniques for making white sauces, souffle bases, gravies, and dessert sauces.

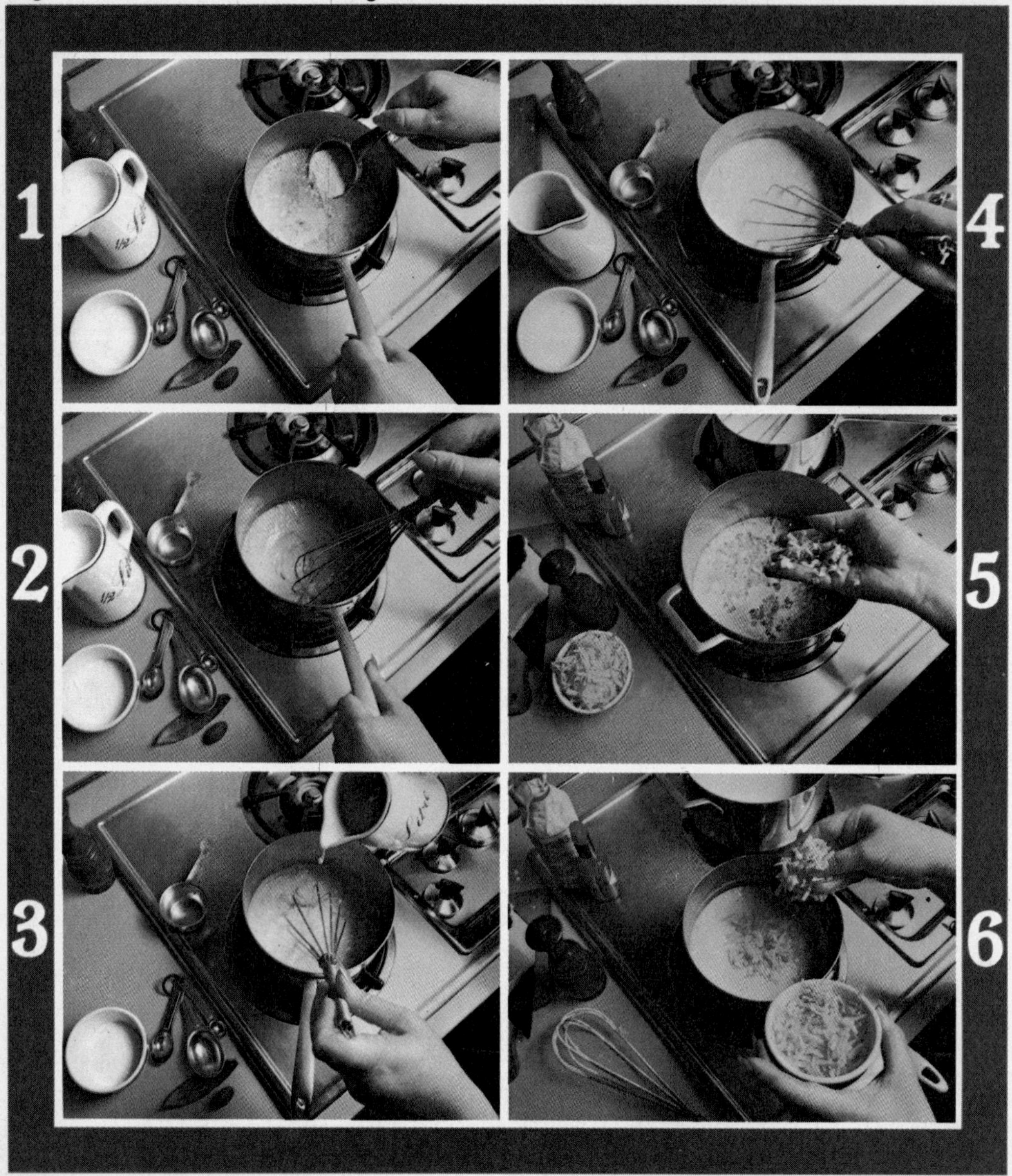

1. Melt butter or margarine until bubbly in a heavy saucepan over medium-high heat.
2. Reduce heat, add the flour, salt and other dry seasonings. Stir mixture well with a wire whip until it is smooth and again begins to bubble and cooks 1 minute.
3. Add milk, broth or other liquid and whip briskly until mixture is very smooth.
4. Cook and stir constantly, until the sauce thickens and bubbles 3 minutes.
5. When using leeks, onions, or shallots, add to the saucepan while the butter melts. Sauté, stirring constantly, so that the onions do not brown. If using curry powder or chili powder in a sauce, cook in the hot butter a few minutes before adding flour.
6. Stir shredded cheese or liquid seasonings into the sauce after it has bubbled 3 minutes, just until smooth and well-blended. Cover surface with plastic wrap until ready to serve.

Sweet-and-Spicy Short Ribs

Meat simmers until ever so tender, then chills in its zippy sauce before baking

Bake at 350° for 1 hour.
Makes 4 servings

3 to 4 pounds beef short ribs
1 cup catsup
1 cup water
1 tablespoon cider vinegar
1 tablespoon Worcestershire sauce
1 tablespoon prepared horseradish
1 tablespoon sugar
1 tablespoon dry mustard
1 teaspoon salt
¼ teaspoon pepper
1 bay leaf
2 medium-size onions, sliced

1 Combine short ribs with remaining ingredients, except onions, in large saucepan; cover. Simmer 2 hours, or until tender. Cool, then chill until 1¼ hours before serving time.
2 Skim off all fat and remove any loose bones from ribs; remove bay leaf. Place meat in a 6-cup baking dish; pour sauce over; top with onion slices; cover.
3 Bake in moderate oven (350°) 30 minutes; uncover; baste onions with sauce in dish. Bake 30 minutes longer, or until meat is very tender.

Shepherd's Stew

So fresh-tasting! Leftover cubed meat, simmered in a rich sauce, is served in fluffy potato-carrot nests

Makes 4 servings

2 cups cubed roast lamb
4 tablespoons all-purpose flour
½ teaspoon salt
Dash of pepper
3 tablespoons vegetable oil
1 large onion, chopped (1 cup)
1 can (10½ ounces) condensed beef consommé
½ teaspoon rosemary leaves, crumbled
4 small potatoes, pared
4 large carrots, pared and cut in 1-inch-long pieces
1 package (9 ounces) frozen artichoke hearts

1 Shake lamb with flour, salt and pepper in a paper bag to coat evenly all over.
2 Brown in vegetable oil in a large frying pan; push to one side. Stir onion into drippings and sauté until soft.
3 Stir in consommé and rosemary; cover. Simmer 30 minutes.
4 While meat mixture simmers, cook potatoes and carrots in boiling salted water in a medium-size saucepan 20 minutes, or until tender; drain. Cook artichoke hearts, following label directions; drain. Stir into stew mixture.
5 Put potatoes and carrots through a ricer onto serving plates; hollow each mound with back of spoon to form a nest. Spoon stew mixture into hollows.

Busy-Day Lamb Ragout

Cranberry-apple juice gets the credit for its mellow flavor. Meat needs no beforehand browning, so it's quick to fix

Makes 6 servings

2 pounds lean boneless lamb shoulder
1 can (3 or 4 ounces) sliced mushrooms
2 teaspoons salt
1 teaspoon fines herbes
½ cup bottled cranberry-apple juice
1 cup water
1 package (10 ounces) frozen Fordhook lima beans
2 medium-size yellow squashes, trimmed and cut in 3-inch-long sticks
¼ cup sifted all-purpose flour

1 Trim any fat from lamb; cut lamb into 1-inch cubes. Combine with mushrooms and liquid, salt, herbs, cranberry-apple juice and ½ cup of the water in a kettle or Dutch oven; cover. Heat to boiling.
2 Simmer 1 hour, or until lamb is almost tender. Add frozen lima beans and squashes; cover again. Simmer 30 minutes longer, or until lamb and vegetables are tender.
3 Remove the lamb and vegetables from kettle with a slotted spoon to heated individual serving bowls or soup plates, or one large bowl; keep warm while making gravy.
4 Pour liquid into a 2-cup measure; add water, if needed, to make 2 cups; return to kettle.
5 Blend flour into remaining ½ cup water until smooth in a cup; stir into liquid in kettle. Cook, stirring constantly, until gravy thickens and boils 1 minute; pour over meat mixture. Garnish with watercress and serve with thick slices of crusty French bread, buttered and toasted hard rolls, or sesame-seed wafers, if you wish.

Make-Easy Irish Stew

This delicately seasoned favorite hides two cooking secrets

Makes 6 servings

3 pounds lean shoulder of lamb, cut for stew
2 teaspoons salt
2 bay leaves
4 cups water
2 packages (8 ounces each) frozen onions in cream sauce
1 bag (1½ pounds) frozen whole boiled potatoes
3 tablespoons chopped parsley

1 Combine lamb, salt, bay leaves and water in a kettle or Dutch oven; cover. Heat to boiling, then simmer 1 hour, or until meat almost falls off bones.
2 Lift out meat with a slotted spoon; let cool until easy to handle, then take meat from bones and trim off fat.
3 Let fat rise to top of broth and skim off; remove bay leaves. Return lamb to broth; add onions and potatoes; cover.
4 Heat to boiling, then simmer 45 minutes, or until vegetables are tender. Sprinkle with chopped parsley. Serve in soup plates or shallow bowls.

Lamb Burgundy

French choice, ideal for making ahead—and making your reputation as a cook

Bake at 350° for 1½ hours.
Makes 8 servings

½ pound sliced bacon, cut in 1-inch pieces
3 pounds lean boneless lamb shoulder, cut in 1-inch cubes
½ cup sifted all-purpose flour
2 cups dry red wine
1 can (10½ ounces) condensed beef broth
Water
2 cloves of garlic, crushed
3 teaspoons salt
Few sprigs parsley
1 teaspoon leaf thyme
1 bay leaf
1 package (1 pound) carrots
2 tablespoons butter or margarine
1 teaspoon leaf basil, crumbled
2 packages (10 ounces each) frozen peas, thawed slightly
SKILLET ONIONS *(recipe follows)*
MUSHROOM SAUTÉ *(recipe follows)*

1 Place bacon in a small saucepan; add water to cover. Heat to boiling; remove from heat; let stand 3 minutes. Drain well on paper toweling.
2 Sauté bacon until crisp in a Dutch oven; remove with a slotted spoon and set aside for Step 9
3 Brown lamb, part at a time, in bacon drippings in Dutch oven; return all meat. Sprinkle flour over top; stir to coat meat evenly. Cook, stirring constantly, 2 minutes, or just until flour browns lightly.
4 Stir in wine, beef broth, 1¼ cups water, garlic and 2 teaspoons of the salt; cook, stirring constantly, until sauce thickens and boils 1 minute; remove from heat.
5 Tie parsley, thyme and bay leaf in a small piece of cheesecloth; add to Dutch oven, pushing down into liquid; cover.
6 Bake in moderate oven (350°), stirring several times, 1½ hours, or until lamb is tender.
7 While lamb cooks, pare carrots; slice thin diagonally. Combine with butter or margarine, remaining 1 teaspoon salt, basil and ½ cup water in an 8-cup baking dish; cover.
8 Bake in moderate oven (350°) 30 minutes. Stir in peas; cover again. Bake 30 minutes longer, or until carrots are tender.
9 Stir bacon, SKILLET ONIONS and MUSHROOMS SAUTÉ into lamb mixture. Spoon into a serving dish; spoon part of the carrots and peas around edge. Garnish with fluted mushrooms and serve with remaining carrots and peas.

SKILLET ONIONS—Peel 2 pounds small white onions. Combine with 3 tablespoons butter or margarine in a large frying pan; heat slowly, stirring several times, 10 minutes, or just until onions are lightly browned. Stir in 1 envelope instant chicken broth or 1 chicken-bouillon cube and ½ cup water; heat to boiling; cover. Simmer 45 minutes, or just until onions are tender.

MUSHROOMS SAUTÉ—Lightly wash 1 pound medium-size fresh mushrooms; trim stem ends. To make the fancy fluted ones for garnish: Remove stems from 4 mushrooms, then cut a small triangle in center of each cap with a sharp-tip knife. Starting at these marks, make 8 evenly spaced curved cuts in each, about ⅛ inch deep, to outside edge. Make a second curved cut just behind each line, slanting knife in slightly; lift out the narrow strips. Slice remaining whole mushrooms and stems. Melt 2 tablespoons butter or margarine in a medium-size frying pan; add fluted mushrooms; sauté 2 to 3 minutes, or until tender; remove from pan. Stir in sliced mushrooms and sauté, stirring several times, just until tender.

Spring Lamb Stew with Mint Dumplings

Light, puffy dumplings, perky with fresh mint add a different touch to a lamb stew

Makes 6 servings

- 2 *pounds lamb shoulder, cut in 2-inch cubes*
- 1 *medium-size onion, chopped (½ cup)*
- 2 *cups boiling water*
- *Handful of celery tops*
- 2 *teaspoons salt*
- ¼ *teaspoon pepper*
- 18 *small white onions, peeled*
- 6 *carrots, pared and cut in 1-inch lengths*
- 1 *cup sliced celery*
- 2 *cups biscuit mix*
- 1 *tablespoon chopped fresh mint*
- ¾ *cup milk*

1 Trim meat; brown, a few pieces at a time, in large heavy kettle or Dutch oven, using a few fat trimmings, if needed. Remove meat and set aside. Stir in onion; sauté until golden in same kettle. Return meat to kettle; add boiling water, celery tops, salt and pepper.
2 Cover tightly; simmer 1 hour, or until meat is tender; remove celery tops. Arrange onions, carrots and celery around meat; cover. Simmer 30 minutes longer, or until vegetables are tender.
3 Combine biscuit mix and mint in small bowl; stir in milk just until mixture is moistened.
4 Drop by tablespoonfuls on top of steaming stew. Cook, uncovered, 10 minutes, then cover tightly and cook 10 minutes longer, or until dumplings are puffy-light.

It doesn't have to take long to duplicate a classic recipe. Here, **Lamb Burgundy** is perfect for a make - ahead.

English Hot Pot

Traditionally, mutton is the meat. Our recipe calls for lamb with potatoes, onion and yellow squash

Bake at 350° for 3 hours.
Makes 6 to 8 servings

2 pounds lamb shoulder, cut in 1-inch cubes
¼ cup unsifted all-purpose flour
2 envelopes instant chicken broth
2 teaspoons salt
1 teaspoon leaf oregano, crumbled
½ teaspoon leaf rosemary, crumbled
¼ teaspoon pepper
1 large onion, sliced and separated into rings
3 small yellow squashes, cut in 2-inch pieces
12 small potatoes, pared and halved
1 cup boiling water
2 tablespoons butter or margarine, melted

1 Trim all fat from lamb. Shake cubes, a few at a time, in flour in a paper bag to coat well.
2 Mix instant chicken broth, salt, oregano, rosemary and pepper in a cup.
3 Layer meat and vegetables into a 10-cup deep baking dish this way: Half of each of lamb, onion and squash, sprinkling each layer lightly with seasoning mixture. Repeat with remaining lamb, vegetables and seasonings.
4 Lay potatoes, rounded side up, on top; pour boiling water over. Brush potatoes with butter or margarine; cover.
5 Bake in moderate oven (350°) 2½ hours, or until lamb is tender; uncover; brush potatoes with more butter, if you wish. Bake 30 minutes longer, or until potatoes are golden-brown.

Dutch Pork Hot Pot

Vegetable choices to go with the succulent pork are red kidney beans, potatoes, onions and carrots

Bake at 350° for 3 hours.
Makes 6 to 8 servings

2 pounds boneless pork shoulder, cut in 1-inch cubes
¼ cup unsifted all-purpose flour
3 teaspoons salt
1 teaspoon leaf thyme, crumbled
1 teaspoon coriander seeds, crushed
¼ teaspoon pepper
1 can (about 1 pound) red kidney beans
Boiling water
4 medium-size potatoes, pared and cut into ¼-inch-thick slices
4 medium-size onions, sliced and separated into rings
8 carrots, pared and cut in 4-inch lengths
2 tablespoons butter or margarine

1 Trim all fat from pork. Shake cubes, a few at a time, with flour in a paper bag to coat well.
2 Mix salt, thyme, coriander and pepper in a cup.
3 Drain liquid from kidney beans into a 2-cup measure; add boiling water to make 1½ cups.
4 Layer vegetables and meat into a 12-cup deep baking dish this way: Half of each of potatoes, onions, pork, kidney beans and carrots, sprinkling each layer lightly with seasoning mixture. Repeat with remaining vegetables, pork and seasoning mixture.
5 Pour liquid over; dot with butter or margarine; cover.
6 Bake in moderate oven (350°) 3 hours, or until pork is tender.

Harvest Pork Bake

Meat, sweet potatoes and apples bake together for this inviting main course in one dish

Bake at 350° for 30 minutes.
makes 6 servings

2 pounds boneless lean pork shoulder, cut in 1-inch cubes
2 tablespoons vegetable oil
2 large onions, chopped (2 cups)
2 tablespoons all-purpose flour
1½ teaspoons salt
1 teaspoon leaf basil, crumbled
1 teaspoon leaf rosemary, crumbled
¼ teaspoon pepper
2 envelopes instant chicken broth
2 cups water
4 medium-size sweet potatoes
3 medium-size apples, pared, quartered, cored and sliced

1 Brown pork cubes, a few at a time, in vegetable oil in a large saucepan; remove. Add onions and sauté just until soft, then return pork to pan.
2 Mix flour, salt, basil, rosemary, pepper and instant chicken broth in a cup; sprinkle over meat mixture; toss to mix. Stir in water slowly; cover.
3 Heat to boiling, then simmer 2 hours, or until meat is tender.

4 While meat cooks, parboil sweet potatoes in boiling salted water in a medium-size saucepan 20 minutes. Drain, then peel; cut in ¼-inch-thick slices.
5 Set aside a few sweet-potato and apple slices for top, then layer remaining into an 8-cup baking dish. Pour hot meat mixture over; arrange saved sweet-potato and apple slices on top; cover.
6 Bake in moderate oven (350°) 30 minutes, or until sweet potatoes and apples are tender.

Bavarian Pork and Kraut

This robust combination of pork hocks and sauerkraut is country cooking at its best

Bake at 325° for 1 hour.
Makes 4 servings

4 pork hocks, about ¾ pound each
1 large onion, sliced
1 bay leaf
Handful of celery tops
2 cups cold water
1½ teaspoons salt
¼ teaspoon pepper
1 can (1 pound, 11 ounces) sauerkraut
¼ cup firmly packed brown sugar
1 tart apple, cut in wedges

1 Simmer pork with onion, bay leaf and celery in water 3 hours, or until tender; drain. (Broth makes a delicious base for pea or bean soup.)
2 Place pork in 8-cup baking dish; top with undrained sauerkraut mixed with brown sugar and apple wedges; cover.
3 Bake in slow oven (325°) 1 hour to blend flavors.

Louisiana Hot Pot

As its name suggests, this recipe calls for sweet smoky ham with sunny yams

Bake at 350° for 3 hours.
Makes 6 to 8 servings

2 pounds cook-before-eating ham, cut in 1-inch cubes
¼ cup unsifted all-purpose flour
2 teaspoons salt
1 teaspoon curry powder
¼ teaspoon pepper
6 medium-size yams or sweet potatoes, pared and cut in ¼-inch-thick slices
4 leeks, trimmed and sliced
OR: 2 medium-size onions, sliced
1 pound fresh peas, shelled (1 cup)
OR: 1 package (10 ounces) frozen green peas
¼ cup sliced stuffed olives
2 cups boiling water
2 tablespoons butter or margarine

1 Trim all fat from ham. Shake cubes, a few at a time, with flour in a paper bag to coat well.
2 Mix salt, curry powder and pepper in a cup.
3 Layer vegetables and meat into a 12-cup deep baking dish this way: Half of each of yams or sweet potatoes, leeks or onions, ham, peas and olives, sprinkling each layer lightly with seasoning mixture. Repeat with remaining vegetables, ham and seasoning mixture.
4 Pour boiling water over; dot with butter or margarine; cover.
5 Bake in moderate oven (350°) 3 hours, or until ham is tender.

PRESSURE COOKER SHORT-CUTS

Sometimes cooking a casserole may involve cooking dried beans for a great length of time, longer than you have at hand. You can short-cut this time by precooking them in a 4- to 6-quart pressure cooker.

To do so, soak 1 package (1 pound) dried beans overnight in a large bowl with ¼ cup vegetable oil, 1 tablespoon salt and enough water to cover beans. In the morning, drain beans; place in pressure cooker with enough water to cover. (Important: Never fill pressure cooker more than half way; the beans will gain bulk as they absorb water.) Cover cooker securely; set pressure regulator on vent pipe; cook, according to the table below:

Black Beans	35 minutes
Blackeyed Peas	20 minutes
Great Northern Beans	30 minutes
Kidney Beans	25 minutes
Lentils	20 minutes
Lima Beans	25 minutes
Navy Beans	30 minutes
Pinto Beans	25 minutes

Party Jambalaya is always a crowd-pleaser that can be effortless to make and a joy to eat.

Fish, and Seafood, Eggs, and Cheese

In this chapter, you'll discover a multitude of casseroles that range from four-person meals to company fare—from a simple egg ramekin to a sumptuous jambalaya.

FISH AND SEAFOOD

Party Jambalaya

Here's a fix-early, bake-later version of the famous Deep South specialty combining shrimps, ham, and rice

Bake at 350° for 1 hour.
Makes 8 servings

8 slices bacon
1 large onion, diced (1 cup)
1 large green pepper, halved, seeded, and diced (1 cup)
1 cup diced celery
1 clove garlic, minced
2 cups regular uncooked rice
2 teaspoons sugar
2 teaspoons salt
⅛ teaspoon cayenne
1 teaspoon Worcestershire sauce
1 can (about 1 pound) tomatoes
1 bag (1½ pounds) frozen deveined shelled raw shrimps
1 one-pound canned ham
3½ cups boiling water
1 bay leaf

1 Sauté bacon until almost crisp in a medium-size frying pan, then before removing from pan, roll each slice around the tines of a fork to make a curl; hold in place with a wooden pick, if needed. Drain on paper toweling; set aside for garnish in Step 7.
2 Sauté onion, green pepper, celery, and garlic until soft in drippings in pan; set aside for Step 5.
3 Combine rice, sugar, salt, cayenne, Worcestershire sauce, and tomatoes, breaking up tomatoes with a fork, in a 12-cup baking dish.
4 Pour just enough hot water over shrimps to separate them, then drain and add to rice mixture.
5 Scrape gelatin coating from ham and add to baking dish. Dice ham; stir with onion mixture into baking dish. Cover and chill until 1 hour before serving time.
6 When ready to bake, slowly pour the 3½ cups boiling water into baking dish; stir with a fork to mix well; lay bay leaf on top; cover.
7 Bake in moderate oven (350°) 1 hour, or until rice is tender and almost all liquid is absorbed. Remove bay leaf; fluff up mixture with a fork, pulling a few shrimps to top; garnish with bacon curls and green-pepper rings.

Lobster Supreme

Layers of macaroni and cheese, lobster, and peas stack up to a company dish

Bake at 350° for 30 minutes.
Makes 6 servings

1 package (8 ounces) elbow macaroni
2 cans (about 6 ounces each) lobster meat
1 tablespoon lemon juice
3 tablespoons butter or margarine
3 tablespoons all-purpose flour
1 teaspoon salt
⅛ teaspoon pepper
1½ cups milk
1 cup grated Cheddar cheese
1 teaspoon dry mustard
1 package (10 ounces) frozen peas

1 Cook macaroni in boiling salted water in large saucepan, following label directions; drain; return to kettle.
2 Drain lobster; remove any bony tissue; cut in bite-size pieces in medium-size bowl; sprinkle lemon juice over.
3 Melt butter or margarine in medium-size saucepan; remove from heat; blend in flour, salt, and pepper; slowly stir in milk. Cook, stirring constantly, until sauce thickens and boils 1 minute.
4 Spoon ½ cup sauce over lobster; mix gently.

(continued)

Pour remaining sauce over macaroni; stir in cheese and mustard.
5 Spoon macaroni mixture into a 6-cup greased baking dish; top with lobster mixture; cover.
6 Bake in moderate oven (350°) 30 minutes, or until bubbly-hot.
7 While casserole bakes, cook peas, following label directions; drain. Season with salt, pepper, and butter or margarine, if desired; keep hot. Spoon around edge of casserole just before serving.

Shrimp Newburg Ramekins

Frozen shrimps, soup, and peas star in this inviting meatless-day treat

Bake at 350° for 20 to 30 minutes.
Makes 6 servings

1 can (10¾ ounces) condensed cream of shrimp soup
1½ cups milk
1 tablespoon Worcestershire sauce
1 pound frozen deveined shelled raw shrimps, cooked
3 cups cooked rice
1 package (10 ounces) frozen peas, cooked, drained, and seasoned
6 lemon slices

1 Combine soup, milk, and Worcestershire sauce in a large saucepan; heat slowly, stirring often, until bubbly. Fold in shrimps and rice. Spoon into 6 individual baking dishes or an 8-cup baking dish.
2 Bake in moderate oven (350°) 20 minutes for small baking dishes, or 30 minutes for large one, or until bubbly-hot.
3 Spoon seasoned peas around edge of each dish; garnish with a twist of lemon.

Seafood Lasagna

An easy-serve specialty made with shrimp soup and crab. Fix ahead, ready to bake just before dinnertime

Bake at 350° for 1 hour.
Makes 8 generous servings

½ pound lasagna noodles
1 tablespoon olive oil or vegetable oil
2 cans (10¾ ounces each) condensed cream of shrimp soup
2 cans (about 7 ounces each) king crabmeat
2 cups (1 pound) cream-style cottage cheese
1 package (8 ounces) cream cheese, softened
1 large onion, chopped (1 cup)
1 egg
2 teaspoons leaf basil, crumbled
1 teaspoon salt
¼ teaspoon pepper
4 medium-size ripe tomatoes, peeled and sliced
2 teaspoons sugar
1 cup grated Cheddar cheese (¼ pound)

1 Slide lasagna noodles, a few at a time so as not to break, into a large kettle of boiling salted water. Add olive oil or vegetable oil to keep noodles from sticking. Cook, stirring often with a wooden spoon, 15 minutes, or just until tender. Drain; cover with cold water.
2 While noodles cook, drain and flake crabmeat, carefully removing any thin bony tissue. Combine crabmeat and soup in large saucepan. Heat until bubbly.
3 Blend cottage cheese and cream cheese with onion, egg, basil, salt, and pepper in large bowl.
4 Line bottom of a lightly oiled baking dish, 13x9x2, with a single layer of noodles. (Lift each strip separately from water with tongs and hold over kettle to drain.) Top with half of cheese mixture, another single layer of noodles, then all of crab sauce. Cover with remaining noodles, then remaining cheese mixture. Arrange tomato slices in single layer on top; sprinkle with sugar. (Casserole can be put together up to this point, then chilled. Remove from refrigerator and let stand at room temperature 30 minutes before baking.)
5 Bake in moderate oven (350°) 15 minutes; sprinkle with grated cheese. Bake 45 minutes longer, or until crusty brown. Let stand about 15 minutes to set, then cut in 8 servings; lift out with wide spatula.

Crab Veronique

A choice to please gourmets! Sweet crab blended with green grapes in a creamy sauce bakes atop seasoned rice

Bake at 375° for 20 minutes.
Makes 6 servings

1 cup regular uncooked rice
1 envelope instant vegetable broth OR: 1 vegetable bouillon cube
1¼ cups hot water
½ cup chopped celery
¼ cup chopped parsley
2 cans (about 7 ounces each) crabmeat
4 tablespoons (½ stick) butter or margarine

4 tablespoons all-purpose flour
½ teaspoon salt
1 tall can (14½ ounces) evaporated milk
1 cup apple juice
1 tablespoon lemon juice
1 cup halved seeded green grapes

1 Cook rice in a large saucepan, following label directions; drain; return to pan.
2 Dissolve instant vegetable broth or bouillon cube in hot water in a 2-cup measure; pour over drained rice; stir in celery and parsley.
3 While rice cooks, drain crabmeat; flake and remove bony tissue, if any.
4 Melt butter or margarine in a medium-size saucepan; stir in flour and salt, then cook, stirring constantly, just until bubbly. Stir in evaporated milk; continue cooking and stirring until sauce thickens and boils 1 minute; remove from heat. Stir in apple and lemon juices, then fold in crabmeat and grapes.
5 Divide rice mixture among 6 individual buttered ramekins or baking dishes; spoon crab mixture on top.
6 Bake in moderate oven (375°) 20 minutes, or until bubbly. Garnish with lemon slices, if you wish.

Arroz con Pescado

Rice with fish—popular in Latin America—goes high style with crab, sole, and a speedy curry mix

Bake at 350° for 1 hour.
Makes 6 servings

½ cup frozen chopped onion (from a 12-ounce bag)
1 tablespoon olive oil
1 package (6 ounces) curried rice
1 package (6 ounces) frozen crabmeat, thawed and broken in chunks
½ pound fresh fillets of sole, cut in bite-size pieces
2½ cups water
1 package (9 ounces) frozen cut green beans

1 Sauté onion in olive oil just until soft in a large frying pan; stir in rice and contents of the seasoning packet. Cook, stirring constantly, over low heat just until rice is hot.
2 Spoon half into a shallow 6-cup baking dish to cover bottom; top with half of the crabmeat and sole. Repeat layers, arranging sea foods attractively on top.
3 Stir water into frying pan; heat to boiling; pour over layers in baking dish; cover.
4 Bake in moderate oven (350°) 1 hour, or until rice is tender and liquid is absorbed.
5 While seafood bakes, cook beans and season, following label directions; spoon in a ring on top of seafoods.

FREEZER KNOW-HOW

The freezer compartment of your refrigerator is not a catch-all space for anything you don't know what to do with. Use it properly and it can save you time, money, and give added convenience.

How to make your freezer work for you: *In these days of high utility bills, it is a benefit to your budget to follow these rules to successful home freezing:*
- *Never freeze more than one 4-serving casserole for each cubic foot of freezer space at one time.*
- *Cool hot foods to room temperature before placing in freezer to prevent the freezer from warming up.*
- *Package foods carefully for the freezer. Use plastic containers with tight-fitting lids and allow about ½-inch of headroom for food to expand.*

What if the freezer shuts off: *This may be because there is a power failure, or because your freezer breaks down. Regardless, you have an immediate problem—what to do with the food in the freezer compartment.*
- *Keep freezer door closed tightly—if freezer is fully stocked, the contents will stay frozen for at least two days; if it is half-full, the food will stay frozen for about one day.*
- *For periods longer than a day or two, buy dry ice—25 pounds for each cubic foot of freezer space—and place large chunks (with gloved hands) on top of the food. If the freezer is fully stocked, the dry ice will keep the food frozen three to four days; in a half-filled freezer, the dry ice will keep the food frozen up to two to three days.*
- *If foods have partially thawed, but still have ice crystals in their packages, they can be safely refrozen. To make sure food is only partially thawed (when ice crystals are not discernible), slip a thermometer between the food and its wrapping. If the temperature is 40°F. or lower, the food can be safely refrozen.*
- *If uncooked foods have thawed, cook, then safely refreeze. Any cooked foods should be heated and eaten.*

Asapao de Pescado

In no time at all, you can assemble and bake this casserole and pretend you're in Spain

Bake at 400° for 20 minutes.
Makes 6 servings.

1 clove garlic, minced
2 tablespoons vegetable oil
1 can (1 pound) stewed tomatoes
1 can (13½ ounces) chicken broth
1 package (6 ounces) Spanish rice mix
1 package (10 ounces) frozen Italian Vegetables in sauce
½ teaspoon leaf savory, crumbled
1 package (1 pound) frozen fillet of sole
1 can (1 pint, 8 ounces) steamed clams

1 Sauté garlic in oil in large skillet until soft. Add tomatoes, chicken broth, rice mix, vegetables, and savory. Cover; bring to boiling. Transfer to 8-cup baking dish.
2 Cut sole into 1-inch cubes; add to tomato mixture. Add clams with shells and ½ cup clam liquid. Bake in hot oven (400°) 20 minutes, or until bubbly-hot.

This may look like an Eastern-shore clam bake, but it's not. The clams *are* there and so is sole and tomatoes, but the recipe hails from Sunny Spain where **Asapao de Pescado** has been a favorite for a long time period. And to make the dish ever more international, there are frozen Italian vegetables in a sauce.

Clam Casserole

A quick-to-prepare delicious casserole that will suit any palate

Bake at 350° for 30 minutes.
Makes 4 servings

1 can (about 8 ounces) minced clams
Milk
6 tablespoons (¾ stick) butter or margarine
2 tablespoons all-purpose flour
1 egg
1 cup fine soft bread crumbs (about 2 slices)

1 Drain liquid from clams into a 2-cup measure; add milk to make 1½ cups.
2 Melt half of the butter or margarine in a medium-size saucepan; stir in flour. Cook, stirring constantly, until bubbly. Stir in the 1½ cups milk mixture; continue cooking and stirring until mixture thickens and boils 1 minute; remove from heat; cool. Beat in egg and clams.
4 Melt remaining butter or margarine in a small frying pan; stir in bread crumbs. Heat slowly, shaking pan constantly, until crumbs are lightly toasted. Spoon half into a greased 4-cup baking

(continued)

dish; top with clam mixture; sprinkle with remaining crumb mixture.
4 Bake in moderate oven (350°) 30 minutes, or until heated through.

Scallops Louis

Scallops add a Friday twist to macaroni seasoned with a creamy dressing

Bake at 350° for 15 to 30 minutes.
Makes 6 servings

1 pound fresh or frozen sea scallops
1 teaspoon shrimp spice
1 slice lemon
2 cups water
1 package (8 ounces) elbow macaroni
3 tablespoons butter or margarine
1 cup coarse soft bread crumbs (2 slices)
2 tablespoons all-purpose flour
1 teaspoon dry mustard
½ teaspoon salt
2½ cups milk
¼ cup chili sauce
1 package (4 ounces) shredded Cheddar cheese
3 small tomatoes

1 Wash fresh scallops under running cold water or partly thaw frozen ones; cut into small pieces.
2 Combine shrimp spice, lemon, and water in a medium-size saucepan; heat to boiling; add scallops; cover. Remove from heat; let stand 5 minutes, then drain.
3 Cook macaroni in a kettle, following label directions; drain; return to kettle.
4 While macaroni cooks, melt butter or margarine in a medium-size saucepan; toss 1 tablespoonful with the bread crumbs in a small bowl for Step 6. Stir flour, mustard, and salt into remaining butter in saucepan; cook, stirring constantly, just until bubbly. Stir in milk; continue cooking and stirring until sauce thickens slightly and boils 1 minute; remove from heat, then stir in chili sauce.
5 Pour over macaroni, then stir in scallops. Spoon into 6 individual buttered baking dishes or a buttered 8-cup baking dish; sprinkle with cheese.
6 Cut stem ends from tomatoes; halve tomatoes crosswise and sprinkle lightly with sugar, salt, and pepper, if you wish. Place on top of macaroni mixture; sprinkle buttered crumbs around edges.
7 Bake in moderate oven (350°) 15 minutes for individual baking dishes and 30 minutes for large one, or until browned and bubbly.

Gourmet Sole

A subtle touch of herbs and grapes enhances the delicate flavor of fish fillets in this dish fit for a party

Bake at 350° for 25 minutes.
Makes 4 servings

1 can (10¾ ounces) condensed chicken broth
1 soup can of water
⅛ teaspoon salt
Dash of white pepper
⅛ teaspoon bouquet garni for fish
12 seedless green grapes, halved
1 package (1 pound) frozen fillets of sole, thawed
4 tablespoons (½ stick) butter or margarine
4 tablespoons all-purpose flour
2 tablespoons dry white wine

1 Combine chicken broth, water, salt, pepper, bouquet garni, and grapes in a large frying pan; heat to boiling.
2 Separate fillets; place in pan; cover. Simmer 12 minutes.
3 Lift fillets from liquid with a pancake turner; place in a shallow baking dish. Pour liquid into a 2-cup measure; add water, if needed, to make 2 cups.
4 Melt butter or margarine in a medium-size saucepan; stir in flour. Cook slowly, stirring constantly, until bubbly. Stir in the 2 cups liquid; continue cooking and stirring until sauce thickens and boils 1 minute. Stir in wine; pour over fish.
5 Bake in moderate oven (350°) 25 minutes. Serve with cooked rice.

Baked Seafood Casserole

Shrimp, crab, and cheese bake in a rich sauce for this special-occasion casserole

Bake at 350° for 1 hour.
Makes 4 servings

1 can (5 ounces) deveined shrimps, drained and rinsed

1 can (about 8 ounces) crabmeat, drained and flaked
6 cups cubed French or Italian bread
¼ cup chopped parsley
1 cup diced Cheddar cheese
4 eggs
2 cups milk
1 cup light cream or table cream
4 tablespoons (½ stick) butter or margarine, melted
2 teaspoons dry mustard
½ cup shredded Cheddar cheese

1 Combine shrimps and crabmeat in a medium-size bowl.
2 Combine bread cubes, chopped parsley, and diced cheese in a second bowl. Alternately layer seafood and bread mixtures, a quarter at a time, into a buttered 10-cup baking dish.
3 Beat eggs slightly in a medium-size bowl; stir in milk, cream, melted butter or margarine, mustard, and shredded cheese; pour over layers in dish; chill 1 hour.
4 Bake in moderate oven (350°) 1 hour, or until puffed and golden.

Golden Fish Bake in Cream

Three Scandinavian favorites—fish, dill, and sour cream—make this tempting dish

Bake at 350° for 55 minutes.
Makes 6 servings

2 packages (1 pound each) frozen cod, haddock or flounder fillets, thawed
OR: 2 pounds fresh cod, haddock, or flounder fillets
4 tablespoons all-purpose flour
2 teaspoons salt
¼ teaspoon pepper
1 cup milk
2 cups coarse soft bread crumbs (4 slices)
4 tablespoons (½ stick) butter or margarine
1 teaspoon dillweed
1 cup dairy sour cream
1 lemon, sliced
Parsley

1 Cut frozen or fresh fillets into serving-size pieces; coat with mixture of flour, salt, and pepper. Arrange in single layer in baking dish, 13x9x2; pour milk over.
2 Bake, uncovered, in moderate oven (350°) 45 minutes.
3 Toast crumbs lightly in butter or margarine in medium-size frying pan. Stir dill into sour cream. Remove fish from oven; spoon cream mixture over; top with toasted crumbs.
4 Bake 10 minutes longer, or until sour cream is set. Garnish with lemon slices and parsley; spoon buttered hot green peas at either end of dish, if you wish.

Pie Pacifica

A shattery-crisp pastry "fish" tops this pantry-shelf tuna special

Bake casserole at 400° for 20 to 25 minutes;
pastry for 12 to 15 minutes.
Makes 6 servings

1 can (about 1 pound) green peas
1 can (16 ounces) whole-kernel corn
1 can (10½ ounces) condensed vegetable soup
1 small can evaporated milk (⅔ cup)
2 cans (about 7 ounces each) tuna, drained and broken into chunks
1 can (4 ounces) pimientos, drained and diced
2 teaspoons instant minced onion
1 package piecrust mix

1 Drain liquid from peas and corn into a medium-size saucepan. Stir in soup and evaporated milk; heat to boiling.
2 Combine peas, corn, tuna, pimientos, and onion in shallow 8-cup baking dish; pour boiling soup mixture over; stir to mix.
3 Bake in hot oven (400°) 20 to 25 minutes, or until bubbly-hot.
4 While tuna mixture bakes, make and bake pastry topping: Prepare piecrust mix, following label directions. Place on lightly floured cookie sheet on a damp towel to prevent slipping; roll out to a shape about 1 inch smaller than top of baking dish.
5 Trim edges evenly or, to make a fish design as pictured, cut around a fish shape (cardboard or plate). Mark "scales" by making shallow curved cuts, holding sharp-point knife on a slant.
6 Bake in hot oven (400°) 12 to 15 minutes, or until golden-brown.
7 Slide on top of bubbling tuna mixture. Mark eye with a pea, parsley sprig, or a bit of pimiento.

Baked Tuna Salad

An intriguing variation for an American favorite that needs only a green salad to make a meal

Bake at 350° for 40 minutes.
Makes 6 servings

8 ounces elbow macaroni, cooked and drained
¾ cup mayonnaise
1 tablespoon Worcestershire sauce
1 tablespoon lemon juice
1 cup diced celery
1 small onion, grated
2 tablespoons butter or margarine
1 teaspoon salt
⅛ teaspoon pepper
1 tall can (14½ ounces) evaporated milk
1 can tuna, drained and flaked
¾ cup coarsely crumbled round cheese crackers

1 Combine macaroni, mayonnaise, Worcestershire sauce, and lemon juice in an 8-cup baking dish.
2 Sauté celery and onion in butter or margarine until golden; stir in salt, pepper, and evaporated milk; heat to scalding; stir into macaroni mixture; fold in tuna; sprinkle crumbs on top.
3 Bake in moderate oven (350°) 40 minutes, or until bubbly.

Macaroni-Tuna Mornay

Popular macaroni-and-cheese joins with tuna and golden corn in this casserole

Bake at 350° for 1 hour.
Makes 8 servings

1 package (8 ounces) elbow macaroni
4 tablespoons (½ stick) butter or margarine
1 cup soft bread crumbs (2 slices)
2 tablespoons grated Parmesan cheese
3 tablespoons all-purpose flour
2 teaspoons salt
1 teaspoon dry mustard
¼ teaspoon pepper
3½ cups milk
1 package (8 ounces) Cheddar cheese, grated
1 can (16 ounces) whole-kernel corn, drained
2 cans (about 7 ounces each) tuna, drained and broken into chunks
1 can (3 or 4 ounces) sliced mushrooms

1 Cook macaroni in a kettle, following label directions; drain; return to kettle.
2 While macaroni cooks, melt butter or margarine in a medium-size saucepan; remove from heat. Toss 1 tablespoon with bread crumbs and Parmesan cheese in a small bowl; set aside for Step 4.
3 Stir flour, salt, mustard, and pepper into remaining butter or margarine in saucepan; cook, stirring all the time, just until mixture bubbles. Stir in milk slowly; continue cooking and stirring until sauce thickens and boils 1 minute; stir in Cheddar cheese until melted.
4 Stir corn, tuna, mushrooms and liquid, and cheese sauce into drained macaroni in kettle. Spoon into a 10-cup baking dish; sprinkle with bread crumb-cheese mixture. Cover and chill.
5 One hour before serving time, uncover casserole; place in a cold oven; set heat control at moderate (350°). Bake 1 hour, or until bubbly-hot in center and crumbs are toasted.

Golden Tuna Pie

Refrigerated biscuits are your short-cut helper to its inviting topper

Bake at 425° for 45 minutes.
Makes 6 servings

2 cans (1 pound each) lima beans, drained
2 cans (about 7 ounces each) tuna, drained and flaked
1 can (1 pound) stewed tomatoes
1 tablespoon sugar
½ teaspoon Italian seasoning
1 small package refrigerated plain or buttermilk biscuits
2 tablespoons butter or margarine, melted
¼ cup cornmeal

1 Mix lima beans and tuna with tomatoes, sugar, and Italian seasoning in a 6-cup baking dish.
2 Bake in hot oven (425°) 30 minutes, or until bubbly.
3 While tuna mixture bakes, separate the 6 biscuits; cut a hole in center of each with a doughnut cutter. Roll both large and small circles in melted butter or margarine in a pie plate, then in corn meal to coat well. Arrange on top of tuna mixture.
4 Bake 15 minutes longer, or until biscuits are crusty-golden.

EGGS AND CHEESE

High-Hat Swiss Soufflé

This golden prize literally pops right out of its baker. Recipe tells how to make an excitingly different bonus treat

Bake at 350° for 1 hour.
Makes 6 servings

½ cup (1 stick) butter or margarine
⅔ cup sifted all-purpose flour
1 tablespoon dry mustard
2 teaspoons salt
⅛ teaspoon ground nutmeg
3 cups milk
12 eggs, separated
3 cups grated Swiss cheese (12 ounces)
1 tablespoon finely cut chives

1 Prepare an ungreased 6-cup soufflé or straight-side baking dish and a baking pan, 15x10x1, these ways: Fold a piece of foil, 25 inches long, in half lengthwise; wrap around dish to make a 3-inch stand-up collar; hold in place with a paper clip and string. Grease baking pan; line with wax paper; grease paper; dust lightly with flour.
2 Melt butter or margarine in a medium-size saucepan; stir in flour, mustard, salt, and nutmeg; cook, stirring constantly, just until bubbly. Stir in milk; continue cooking and stirring until sauce thickens and boils 1 minute; remove from heat. Let cool while beating eggs.
3 Beat egg whites just until they form soft peaks in a large bowl.
4 Beat egg yolks in a second large bowl; beat in cooled sauce slowly, then stir in cheese and chives; fold in beaten egg whites.
5 Pour half of mixture (about 6 cups) into prepared soufflé dish and remaining into baking pan. Gently cut a deep circle in mixture in dish about 1 inch in from edge with a rubber spatula. (This gives soufflé a double-puffed top.)
6 Bake in moderate oven (350°) 1 hour, or until puffy-firm and golden on top. Serve at once.

(continued)

Here is creativity at its best: **High-Hat Souffle** and **Ham-and-Cheese Roulade** combine cheese, eggs, meat, and vegetables for succulent casseroles.

7 Cover baking pan with wax paper, then wrap in foil. Label, date, and freeze for HAM-AND-CHEESE ROULADE *(recipe follows)*.

Ham-and-Cheese Roulade

Your freezer dividend: A delicate omeletlike roll with a crunchy ham filling and creamy parsley topper made from High-Hat Swiss Soufflé

Bake at 325° for 50 minutes.
Makes 6 servings

1 frozen omelet (from High-Hat Swiss Soufflé)
4 tablespoons (½ stick) butter or margarine
3 tablespoons all-purpose flour
½ teaspoon salt
Dash of pepper
2 cups milk
2 tablespoons chopped parsley
1 cup chopped celery
1 can (6 ounces) whole mushrooms, drained
1 package (about 5 ounces) sliced boiled ham, chopped coarsely
¼ cup chopped toasted slivered almonds (from a 5-ounce can)
1 tablespoon chopped pimiento
Parsley
½ pimiento, cut in 6 thin strips and rolled

1 About 1 hour before serving, remove omelet from freezer; unwrap.
2 Bake in slow oven (325°) 50 minutes, or until golden-brown and top springs back when lightly pressed with fingertip.
3 While omelet bakes, melt 3 tablespoons of the butter or margarine in a medium-size saucepan; stir in flour, salt, and pepper; cook, stirring constantly, until bubbly. Stir in milk; continue cooking and stirring until sauce thickens and boils 1 minute; stir in chopped parsley. Set aside for Step 5.
4 Sauté celery in remaining 1 tablespoon butter or margarine until soft in a medium-size frying pan; remove from heat.
5 Set aside 6 of the prettiest mushrooms for garnish, then chop remaining and stir into celery mixture with ham, almonds, and chopped pimiento; stir in ½ cup of the parsley sauce.
6 Remove omelet from pan this way: Loosen around edge with a spatula; cover with wax paper or foil. Place a large cookie sheet or tray on top, then quickly turn upside down. Lift off pan; peel off wax paper.
7 Spread ham mixture evenly over omelet. Starting at a short end, roll up, jelly-roll fashion, lifting wax paper or foil as you roll to steady and guide it.
8 Lift onto a serving platter with two wide spatulas. Heat parsley sauce again until hot; spoon about ½ cup over roll. Garnish with saved mushrooms, parsley, and rolled strips of pimiento threaded onto wooden picks, as pictured. Slice roll; serve with remaining sauce.
Note—If baking omelet without freezing, bake in slow oven (325°) 40 minutes, or until golden and top springs back when lightly pressed with fingertip.

Golden Cheese Soufflé

Specialty easily made with Muenster and bacon bits looks like a masterpiece

Bake at 350° for 45 minutes.
Makes 6 servings

6 slices bacon, diced
3 tablespoons all-purpose flour
½ teaspoon salt
½ teaspoon dry mustard
1 cup milk
Few drops liquid red pepper seasoning
1 cup shredded Muenster cheese (4 ounces)
6 eggs, separated
¼ cup chopped parsley

1 Sauté bacon until crisp in a small heavy saucepan; remove with a slotted spoon and drain on paper toweling. Pour off all drippings, then measure 3 tablespoonfuls and return to pan.
2 Blend in flour, salt, and mustard; cook, stirring constantly, just until bubbly.
3 Stir in milk and liquid red pepper seasoning; continue cooking and stirring until sauce thickens and boils 1 minute. Stir in cheese until melted; remove from heat. Let mixture cool while beating eggs.
4 Beat egg whites just until they form soft peaks in a medium-size bowl. Beat egg yolks until creamy-thick in a large bowl; blend in cooled cheese sauce, bacon, and parsley; fold in beaten egg whites until no streaks of white remain. Pour into an ungreased 8-cup soufflé or straight-side baking dish.
5 Bake in moderate oven (350°) 45 minutes, or until puffy-firm and golden-brown on top. Serve at once.

HOW TO BUY CHEESE

Buy often and only what you can use in a short time is a good rule to carry with you into the supermarket or grocery store. Cheese is perishable, and that extra cheese you purchase because it looks good often turns out to be stale by the time you cut off a wedge.

But there are other points to bear in mind: Largest packages are generally your thriftiest buys; aged cheese is highest in price; and, while packaged sliced, shredded, cubed, and grated cheese cost a bit more, they often are worth the additional cost in convenience.

Also, know the different types of cheeses that are available. (Elsewhere in this chapter is a list of the kinds of cheeses.)

Natural cheeses: *These are the naturally aged or ripened cheeses. Flavors range from mild to sharp to extra sharp. Recognize them by their individual names, Cheddar, for example.*

Pasteurized process cheese: *These are blends of fresh and aged natural cheeses that have been shredded and heated (hence pasteurized) to stop any further ripening. Buy it sliced, in transparent envelopes, or in blocks, or in ½- to 2-pound loaves. Popular-priced, these are perfect for cooking or making sandwiches.*

Pasteurized process cheese foods: *Made the same way as process cheese, these have nonfat dry milk added. Milder and softer, they melt faster than process cheeses. Look for them in packages as slices, rolls, or links and loaves.*

Pasteurized process cheese spreads: *These are similar to process cheese foods, but they spread more easily because they contain more moisture. There are varieties to please every taste. They're conveniently packaged in jars and loaves —even tubes and pressurized cans—for sandwiches and sauces.*

Queen's Cheese Soufflé

Cream and cottage cheeses, sparked with snips of chives and parsley, make this double-puff beauty

Bake at 350° for 45 minutes.
Makes 6 servings

3 tablespoons butter or margarine
3 tablespoons all-purpose flour
1 teaspoon salt
1 cup milk
Few drops liquid red pepper seasoning
1 package (3 or 4 ounces) cream cheese, softened
½ cup cream-style cottage cheese
1 tablespoon chopped parsley
1 teaspoon finely cut chives
OR: 1 teaspoon freeze-dried chopped chives
6 eggs, separated

1 Melt butter or margarine in a medium-size saucepan; stir in flour and salt; cook, stirring constantly, just until bubbly. Stir in milk and liquid red pepper seasoning; continue cooking and stirring until sauce thickens and boils 1 minute.
2 Beat in cream and cottage cheeses, then stir in parsley and chives; remove from heat; let cool while beating eggs.
3 Beat egg whites just until they form soft peaks in a large bowl.
4 Beat egg yolks until creamy-thick in a second large bowl; blend in cooled cheese sauce; fold in beaten egg whites until no streaks of white remain. Pour into an ungreased 8-cup soufflé or straight-side baking dish; gently cut a deep circle in mixture about 1 inch in from edge with a rubber spatula. (This gives soufflé its double-puffed top.)
5 Bake in moderate oven (350°) 45 minutes, or until puffy-firm and golden on top. Serve at once.

Double Choice Soufflé

Your family has a choice in this soufflé—ham or spinach, or both—in a well-seasoned cheese mixture

Bake at 300° for 1 hour and 15 minutes.
Makes 4 servings

6 tablespoons (¾ stick) butter or margarine
6 tablespoons all-purpose flour
½ teaspoon salt
¼ teaspoon dry mustard
⅛ teaspoon pepper
½ teaspoon onion salt
1½ cups milk
4 ounces Cheddar cheese, shredded (1 cup)
6 eggs, separated
½ cup finely chopped cooked ham
½ cup well-drained cooked spinach, finely chopped

1 Prepare an ungreased 5-cup soufflé or straight-side baking dish this way: Fold a piece

(continued)

of foil 2 inches longer than outside measurement of dish in half lengthwise; wrap around dish to make 3-inch stand-up collar. Hold foil in place with string and paper clip. Take a second piece of foil, about 12 inches long, and fold in half crosswise. Reserve.
2 Melt butter or margarine in a medium-size saucepan; stir in flour, salt, dry mustard, pepper and onion salt; cook, stirring constantly, just until mixture bubbles. Stir in milk slowly; continue cooking and stirring until sauce thickens and bubbles 1 minute. Remove from heat.
3 Stir in cheese, just until melted; let cool while beating eggs.
4 Beat egg whites in a medium-size bowl just until they form soft peaks.
5 Beat egg yolks in a large bowl until thick and fluffy; beat in cooled cheese mixture, a small amount at a time, until blended. Measure out one cup of mixture into a medium-size bowl; stir in ham. Stir spinach into mixture remaining in the other bowl. Beat about ¼ cup of egg white into each bowl to loosen up mixture. Carefully fold in remaining egg whites, dividing evenly between both bowls, until no streaks of white remain.
6 Holding the 6-inch piece of foil in place in the center of the prepared soufflé dish, carefully spoon the ham mixture into one side of the dish and the spinach mixture on the other side. Slowly and carefully pull the piece of foil out.
7 Bake in slow oven (300°) 1 hour and 15 minutes, or until puffy-firm and golden. Serve at once.

Mushroom Soufflé

High in size, this souffle will register high on your guests' pleasure chart

Bake at 350° for 45 minutes.
Makes 6 servings

½ pound fresh mushrooms, washed, trimmed, and chopped
4 tablespoons (½ stick) butter or margarine
3 tablespoons all-purpose flour
½ teaspoon salt
1 cup milk
6 eggs, separated
¼ teaspoon cream of tartar
GRUYÈRE SAUCE *(recipe follows)*

1 Sauté mushrooms in 1 tablespoon of the butter or margarine in a medium-size frying pan 5 minutes; remove from heat.
2 Melt remaining 3 tablespoons butter or margarine in a medium-size saucepan. Blend in flour and salt; cook, stirring constantly, until bubbly. Stir in milk; continue cooking and stirring until sauce thickens and boils 1 minute. Cool while beating eggs.
3 Beat egg whites with cream of tartar just until they form soft peaks in a large bowl.
4 Beat egg yolks until creamy-thick in a second large bowl; blend in cooled sauce, then mushroom mixture. Lightly stir in about 1 cupful of the beaten egg whites, then fold in remainder until no streaks of white remain. Pour into an ungreased 8-cup soufflé or straight-side baking dish; gently cut a deep circle in mixture about an inch in from edge with a rubber spatula. (This gives soufflé its double-puffed top.)
5 Bake in moderate oven (350°) 45 minutes, or until puffy-firm and golden. Serve at once with GRUYÈRE SAUCE.

GRUYÈRE SAUCE—Melt 1 tablespoon butter or margarine in a small saucepan; blend in 1 tablespoon flour, ⅛ teaspoon salt, and ⅛ teaspoon paprika. Cook, stirring constantly, until bubbly. Stir in 1 cup milk; continue cooking and stirring until sauce thickens and boils 1 minute. Cut 3 wedges (1 ounce each) process Gruyére cheese into small pieces; stir into sauce until melted. Stir in 1 tablespoon chopped parsley. Makes about 1⅓ cups.

Avocado Soufflé with Fondue Sauce

Avocado, Swiss cheese, and mushrooms make a most delicate flavor blend

Bake at 375° about 50 minutes.
Makes 6 servings

Soufflé

6 eggs
1 large ripe avocado
4 tablespoons (½ stick) butter or margarine
¼ cup sifted all-purpose flour
½ teaspoon salt
Few drops liquid red pepper seasoning
1 teaspoon minced onion
1 cup milk

Fondue Sauce

2 tablespoons butter or margarine
2 tablespoons all-purpose flour
¼ teaspoon salt
¼ teaspoon pepper
1 cup milk
1 can (3 or 4 ounces) sliced mushrooms
1 cup (4 ounces) freshly grated process Swiss cheese

Mirror, mirror on the wall, what's the most adaptable dish of all? It's a versatile **Quiche Lorraine,** served equally well as an appetizer or as a luncheon entreé.

1 Make soufflé: Separate eggs, putting whites into medium-size bowl, yolks into large bowl.
2 Peel, pit, and mash avocado by pressing through a sieve with a wooden spoon.
3 Melt butter or margarine in medium-size saucepan; remove from heat; blend in flour, salt, liquid red pepper seasoning, and onion; slowly stir in milk. Cook over low heat, stirring constantly, until sauce thickens and boils 1 minute; remove from heat. Blend in avocado; cool.
4 Beat egg whites just until stiff enough to hold their shape but still moist.
5 Beat egg yolks well; slowly stir in cooled avocado mixture; lightly fold in beaten whites until no streaks of sauce or egg white remain; pour into ungreased deep 6-cup baking dish.
6 Bake in moderate oven (375°) 50 minutes, or until top is firm and golden; *serve at once* with hot FONDUE SAUCE.
7 While soufflé bakes, make sauce: Melt butter or margarine in small heavy saucepan; remove from heat; blend in flour, salt, and pepper; slowly stir in milk, mushrooms and liquid, and cheese. Cook over low heat, stirring constantly, until sauce thickens and boils 1 minute.

Quiche Lorraine

A perennial favorite of all who want to display their cooking skills

Bake at 450° for 15 minutes, then at 350° for 15 minutes.
Makes 6 servings

½ package piecrust mix
6 slices bacon
1 medium-size onion, chopped (½ cup)
8 ounces Swiss cheese, shredded (2 cups)
4 eggs
2 cups milk
1 teaspoon salt
¼ teaspoon ground nutmeg
⅛ teaspoon pepper

1 Prepare piecrust mix, following label directions, or make your own single-crust pastry recipe. Roll out to a 12-inch round on a lightly floured pastry board; fit into a 9-inch pie plate or fluted quiche dish. Trim overhang to ½ inch; turn under, flush with rim; flute to make a stand-up edge. Prick shell well all over with a fork. (For quiche dish, level pastry so as to be even with rim.)
2 Bake in hot oven (425°) 5 minutes; remove to wire rack; cool slightly. Increase temperature to 450°.

(continued)

3 Fry bacon in small skillet until crisp; drain all but 1 tablespoon fat; crumble bacon.
4 Sauté onion in bacon fat until soft. Sprinkle cheese evenly in a layer in partly baked pastry shell; add bacon and onion.
5 Beat eggs slightly in a medium-size bowl; slowly beat in milk, salt, nutmeg and pepper; then pour into pastry shell.
6 Bake in hot oven (450°) 15 minutes; lower oven temperature to moderate (350°) for 15 minutes; or until center is almost set but still soft. (Do not overbake, for custard will set as it cools.) Let stand 15 minutes before serving; cut into wedges.

Swiss Custard

It's a spoon-up twist on favorite cheese pie with smoky bacon chips

Bake at 350° for 25 minutes.
Makes 4 servings

4 slices bacon
1½ cups light cream or table cream
1 teaspoon grated onion
4 eggs
½ teaspoon salt
Dash of cayenne
1½ cups shredded Swiss cheese (6 ounces)

1 Cut bacon into 1-inch pieces; sauté until almost crisp in a medium-size frying pan; remove and drain on paper toweling.
2 Scald cream with onion in a small saucepan. Beat eggs slightly with salt and cayenne in a medium-size bowl; stir in cream mixture slowly.
3 Sprinkle cheese in an even layer in a greased shallow 6-cup baking dish; pour egg mixture on top; sprinkle with bacon.
4 Bake in moderate oven (350°) 25 minutes, or until custard is set.

Cheese Custard Fiesta

It's mildly seasoned, creamy, and hearty with plenty of cheese, eggs, and vegetables

Bake at 350° for 50 minutes.
Makes 4 to 6 servings

2 packages (10 ounces each) frozen mixed vegetables
2 cups milk
1 tablespoon grated onion
1 teaspoon dried parsley flakes
½ teaspoon salt
3 drops liquid red pepper seasoning
4 eggs
1 package (8 ounces) process American cheese, shredded

1 Cook mixed vegetables, following label directions; drain. Spoon into a 6-cup baking dish.
2 Scald milk with onion, parsley flakes, salt, and liquid red pepper seasoning in a small saucepan.
3 Beat eggs slightly in a medium-size bowl; slowly stir in milk mixture.
4 Sprinkle cheese over vegetables in baking dish; pour egg mixture over top. Set dish in a baking pan on oven shelf; pour boiling water into pan to a depth of about an inch.
5 Bake in moderate oven (350°) 50 minutes, or until set in center.

Cheddar Puff

Bread and cheese bake and puff to golden perfection for a satisfying main dish

Bake at 350° for 1 hour.
Makes 6 servings

8 slices white bread
3 tablespoons butter or margarine, softened
½ pound sharp Cheddar cheese, grated (2 cups)
4 eggs
2½ cups milk
2 tablespoons prepared mustard
1 teaspoon Worcestershire sauce
½ teaspoon salt
⅛ teaspoon paprika

1 Spread bread with butter or margarine, then cut into large cubes. Place about one third in an 8-cup baking dish.
2 Sprinkle with one third of the cheese; repeat with remaining bread and cheese to make 2 more layers of each.
3 Beat eggs with milk, mustard, Worcestershire sauce, salt, and paprika in a medium-size bowl; pour over bread-cheese layers; cover. Chill at least 3 hours or even overnight.
4 Bake, uncovered, in moderate oven (350°) 1 hour, or until puffed and golden. Let stand 10 minutes to cool slightly before serving.

POPULAR CHEESE KNOW-HOW

Know your cheese and you can enjoy a variety of delicate and robust flavors. There are bold cheeses that work well in appetizer salads, and mild blends that are best between two slices of bread, and cheeses whose robust flavor works well with crackers or fruit, after a meal. Study the list below, and you'll vastly improve your knowledge of cheeses and greatly enhance your enjoyment of this natural food.

KIND	DESCRIPTION	FLAVOR	USES
CHEDDAR	**Semihard with a cream to orange color. Comes as wedges, blocks, cubes, slices, grated.**	**Mild to sharp, depending on aging. Always clearly marked on the package.**	**America's all-round choice for sandwiches, cooked dishes, salads, snacks, desserts.**
SWISS	**Light creamy yellow with large uneven holes. Buy sliced or in cuts.**	**Mild with a nutlike sweetness. One of our most popular cheeses.**	**Same as Cheddar, but in cooked dishes it may "string" somewhat.**
COTTAGE RICOTTA CREAM	**Cottage and ricotta— creamy-white and curdlike. Cream cheese is velvety smooth.**	**All are delicately mild. Easily spoonable and spreadable.**	**Perfect for appetizers, sandwiches, cooked dishes, desserts, cake fillings or frostings.**
BLUE ROQUEFORT GORGONZOLA STILTON	**Medium-soft with blue to blue-green veins. Crumble easily.**	**Mild to tangy, slightly peppery.**	**Give a gourmet touch to appetizers, salads, dressings, desserts.**
EDAM GOUDA	**Creamy orange with red-wax coat. Edam is round; Gouda is flattish.**	**Mellow, slightly salty, with a nutlike taste.**	**Excellent for appetizer and dessert trays. Good snack cheese, too.**
CAMEMBERT BRIE	**Rounds and wedges have an edible gray-white crust, soft inside.**	**Mild to pungent, depending on age.**	**Favorite for desserts and appetizers. Serve at room temperature.**
MOZZARELLA	**Soft and white with a ball-like shape. Also comes sliced or grated.**	**Mild and a bit chewy to eat, especially when heated.**	**Known as the pizza-lasagna cheese. Melts to creamy smoothness quickly.**
MUENSTER BRICK	**Creamy yellow to white, semisoft with tiny holes.**	**Muenster is pungent; brick, mild to sharp.**	**Appetizers, sandwiches, salads, desserts.**
PROVOLONE	**Light brown outside; light yellow inside. Sometimes lined with rope marks.**	**Mellow to sharp, smoky and salty.**	**Try it in macaroni and spaghetti dishes, for sandwiches, snacks, or appetizer trays.**
PARMESAN ROMANO SAP SAGO	**The grating cheeses. Very hard white to light green. Sold in blocks, and grated.**	**Parmesan is pungent, but milder than Romano. Sap Sago has an herb-like flavor.**	**Topper for casserole dishes and spaghetti. Also popular for sauces and vegetable seasoners.**

Italian Potato Puff

For a distinctively different, tasty dish, choose this potato-cheese specialty

Bake at 350° for 30 minutes.
Makes 4 servings

1 small green pepper, seeded and chopped (½ cup)
1 medium-size onion, chopped (½ cup)
3 tablespoons butter or margarine
4 cups prepared instant mashed potatoes
2 tablespoons seasoned dry bread crumbs
1 package (8 ounces) mozzarella cheese, thinly sliced

1 Sauté green pepper and onion in 2 tablespoons of the butter or margarine until soft in a small skillet. Stir into mashed potatoes in a medium-size bowl.
2 Grease a 6-cup round baking dish evenly with the remaining 1 tablespoon butter or margarine. Sprinkle with bread crumbs, making sure to cover inside of dish completely.
3 Layer potatoes and cheese in dish, beginning and ending with potatoes.
4 Bake in moderate oven (350°) 30 minutes, or until potatoes are slightly golden. Turn out onto warm serving dish, shaking gently to loosen. Serve at once.

Canadian Macaroni and Cheese

This oven version calls for a peppy sauce of tomatoes with cheese and herbs. More cheese is sprinkled on top

Bake at 350° for 50 minutes.
Makes 6 servings

1 package (8 ounces) elbow macaroni
1 small onion, chopped
2 tablespoons butter or margarine
1 can (1 pound, 4 ounces) tomatoes
1 cup shredded sharp Cheddar cheese (4 ounces)
½ teaspoon salt
½ teaspoon leaf basil, crumbled
¼ teaspoon pepper

1 Cook macaroni in boiling salted water in a kettle, following label directions; drain; spoon into an 8-cup baking dish.
2 Sauté onion lightly in butter or margarine in a large frying pan; stir in tomatoes, ½ cup of cheese, and seasonings. Heat, stirring, just until cheese melts. Stir into macaroni; sprinkle with remaining cheese.
3 Bake in moderate oven (350°) 50 minutes, or until hot.

Double-Good Macaroni and Cheese

Cream cheese and sour cream bring a new and delightful touch to an old favorite

Bake at 350° for 45 minutes.
Makes 8 servings

1 package (8 ounces) elbow macaroni
1 container (1 pound) cream-style cottage cheese
¾ cup dairy sour cream
1 egg, slightly beaten
1 teaspoon salt
⅛ teaspoon pepper
2 teaspoons grated onion
1 package (8 ounces) sharp Cheddar cheese, shredded

1 Cook macaroni, following label directions; drain.
2 Combine cottage cheese, sour cream, egg, salt, pepper, onion, and Cheddar cheese in a large bowl; mix lightly until blended; fold in macaroni. Spoon into a baking dish, 9x9x2.
3 Bake in moderate oven (350°) 45 minutes, or until bubbly.

Baked Crab-Tuna Fondue

What a joy of a make-ahead, and it's special enough for a party

Bake at 350° for 1 hour and 15 minutes.
Makes 6 servings

1 can (about 7 ounces) crabmeat
1 can (about 4 ounces) tuna
5 cups cubed French bread (about 10 one-inch-thick slices)
1 package (8 ounces) Muenster cheese, cubed
2 tablespoons chopped parsley
4 eggs
3 cups milk

3 tablespoons butter or margarine, melted
2 teaspoons dry mustard
1 teaspoon grated onion

1 Drain crabmeat; flake and remove bony tissue, if needed. Drain and flake tuna. Combine crab and tuna in a small bowl.
2 Layer one-third each of the bread, sea food, cheese, and parsley into a buttered 6-cup straight-side baking dish. Repeat with remaining bread, seafood, cheese, and parsley to make 2 more layers.
3 Beat eggs with milk, melted butter or margarine, mustard, and onion until blended in a medium-size bowl; pour over bread-seafood layers; cover. Chill at least 3 hours, or overnight.

Swiss Puff

Potatoes, cheese, and eggs make this soufflé-like supper dish extra satisfying

Bake at 375° for 40 minutes.
Makes 6 servings

4 eggs, separated
4 cups seasoned hot mashed potatoes
2 cups grated Swiss cheese
2 tablespoons finely cut chives
2 tablespoons chopped parsley
2 tablespoons diced pimiento
Few drops liquid red pepper seasoning

1 Beat egg whites just until they form soft peaks in a large bowl.
2 Beat egg yolks, one at a time, into hot mashed potatoes in a second large bowl; stir in cheese, chives, parsley, pimiento, and liquid red pepper seasoning. Fold in beaten egg whites until no streaks of white remain; spoon into a buttered 6-cup baking dish.
3 Bake in moderate oven (375°) 40 minutes, or until puffed and golden. Serve at once.

Noodle-Egg Bake

It's quick to fix and heat, and just hearty enough for supper

Bake at 350° for 20 minutes.
Makes 4 servings

2 cups (half an 8-ounce package) fine noodles
1 can (10¾ ounces) condensed cream of celery soup
¼ cup milk
¼ cup mayonnaise or salad dressing
1 teaspoon Worcestershire sauce
6 hard-cooked eggs, shelled and sliced
3 tablespoons grated Parmesan cheese

1 Cook noodles, following label directions; drain. Place in a greased shallow 4-cup baking dish.
2 Combine celery soup, milk, mayonnaise or salad dressing, and Worcestershire sauce in a small saucepan; heat slowly, stirring constantly, until smooth and hot; stir half into noodles.
3 Place egg slices over noodle mixture; spoon remaining sauce over eggs. Sprinkle Parmesan cheese on top.
4 Bake in moderate oven (350°) 20 minutes, or until bubbly.

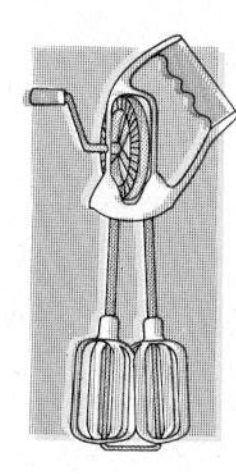

Deviled Egg Bake

Eggs join rice ahd shrimps in creamy soup-sauce for a speedy supper

Bake at 350° for 15 minutes.
Makes 6 servings

6 hard-cooked eggs, shelled
¼ cup mayonnaise or salad dressing
2 teaspoons prepared mustard
¼ teaspoon salt
1 can (5 ounces) deveined shrimps
1 can (10¾ ounces) condensed cream of shrimp soup
½ cup milk
4 cups hot cooked rice

1 Halve eggs crosswise; remove yolks and mash in a small bowl. Blend in mayonnaise or salad dressing, mustard, and salt; pile back into whites.
2 Drain shrimps and rinse. Combine shrimps with soup and milk in a medium-size saucepan. Heat slowly, stirring several times, just until bubbly.
3 Spoon rice into a 6-cup shallow baking dish; arrange stuffed eggs in rows on top, pushing down into rice; spoon shrimp sauce over all.
4 Bake in moderate oven (350°) 15 minutes, or until bubbly-hot. Garnish with parsley, if you wish.

Create 1,294

Meat • Eggs • Cheese • Fish	Potatoes • Pasta • Rice • Beans	Vegetables (fresh or frozen)
Cooked beef or pork: 2 cups diced roast beef 8 to 12 slices meatloaf 2 cups diced fresh pork 12 slices roast pork loin	2 cups mashed potatoes 2 cans (1 pound each) kidney beans, drained 3 cups cooked kasha or bulgar wheat	1 package (9 ounces) frozen green beans with sliced mushrooms, cooked 2 cups sliced cooked carrots 1 large onion, thinly sliced
Cooked chicken or lamb: 2 cups diced chicken 12 slices roast turkey 2 cups diced lamb shoulder 12 slices roast leg of lamb	1 package (6 ounces) chicken-flavored stuffing mix, cooked 3 cups cooked noodles 3 cups cooked white rice	1 can (6 ounces) or ½ pound fresh sliced mushrooms 2 cups cooked sliced celery 1 package (10 ounces) frozen peas, cooked
Cooked ham or sausage: 2 cups diced pork butt 12 slices baked ham 1 pound frankfurters, scored 4 knockwurst, sliced	2 cans (1 pound each) dried lima beans, drained 1 package (1 pound) frozen crinkle-cut French fries 3 cups cooked spaghetti	2 zucchini, diced and cooked 1 can (12 or 16 ounces) whole-kernel corn, drained 2 large red or green peppers, chopped and sautéed
Eggs or cheese: 8 hard-cooked eggs, sliced 2 cups diced Cheddar cheese 8 ounces sliced Swiss cheese 2 cups shredded Gruyère cheese	3 cups cooked brown rice 2 cups peeled and sliced boiled potatoes 3 cups cooked ziti, rotelle or elbow macaroni	1 package (10 ounces) frozen chopped spinach, thawed 2 large onions, chopped and sautéed (2 cups) 2 cups frozen carrots, cooked
Fish or shellfish: 2 cans (about 7 ounces each) tuna 1 can (1 pound) salmon 2 cans (8 ounces each) minced clams 2 cans (5½ ounces each) shrimp	1 package (7 ounces) chicken-flavored rice mix, cooked 1 package (1 pound) frozen macaroni and cheese, thawed 3 cups diced cooked potatoes	2 large cucumbers, pared, cubed and cooked 5 minutes 1 package (9 ounces) frozen Italian green beans, thawed 2 cups cooked diced broccoli

Casseroles

Take one ingredient from each category (read across) and combine them with each other in an 8-cup casserole. Bake in moderate oven (375°) 35 minutes, or until bubbly. Makes 4 to 6 servings.

Sauces and Seasonings	Casserole Toppings
1 can condensed cream of onion soup plus ½ cup milk and 1 teaspoon leaf thyme (crumbled). 2 envelopes (1 ounce) brown gravy mix (prepared) and 2 tablespoons dry red wine. 2 cups bottled barbecue sauce.	Thick tomato slices topped with grated Romano cheese and leaf oregano. Crushed whole-wheat cracker crumbs. Packaged herb-flavored croutons, tossed with melted butter or margarine.
1 package (10 ounces) frozen broccoli spears with hollandaise sauce (cooked). 2 envelopes (1 ounce) white sauce mix (cooked) plus 1 teaspoon curry powder and ¼ cup raisins. 1 can (11 ounces) chicken gravy.	Chinese noodles and sliced water chestnuts. Dry bread crumbs tossed with melted butter or margarine and lemon-pepper. Crushed corn flakes tossed in butter or margarine with chopped chives.
1 can condensed Cheddar cheese soup plus ½ cup beer and 1 tablespoon prepared mustard. 1 envelope spaghetti sauce mix (cooked). 1 package (9 ounces) frozen small onions with cream sauce plus 1 tablespoon chopped parsley.	Shredded process American or Muenster cheese. Crushed corn chips with sliced pitted ripe olives and chopped onion. Wheat germ tossed with melted butter or margarine, chopped parsley and green onions.
1 can (1 pound) stewed tomatoes. ¾ cup mayonnaise or salad dressing plus ½ cup milk and 2 tablespoons lemon juice. 1 envelope (1 ounce) onion sauce mix (cooked) plus ½ teaspoon leaf savory (crumbled).	Canned French fried potato sticks. Soft white bread crumbs tossed in butter or margarine and grated Parmesan cheese. Buttered cherry tomato slices with mixed Italian herbs.
1 package (8 ounces) frozen peas with cream sauce (cooked). 2 envelopes (cup-size) instant lobster bisque plus 1 cup boiling water and 2 tablespoons dry sherry. 1 cup sour cream and ½ cup milk.	Buttered popcorn tossed with seasoned salt and seasoned pepper. Frozen French fried onion rings or potatoes sprinkled with herb-seasoned salt. Toasted slivered almonds.

A just-right blending of beef, noodles, and vegetables, **Teriyaki Casserole** is a flavorful variation of a popular exotic dish that first tempted palates in Japan.

International Crockery Pot Favorites

The newest form of casserole cooking, in an electric slow cooker, deserves a special section—and to make this chapter even more special, we've selected a potpourri of favorites from around the world, all of which serve to improve your culinary skills and increase your repertoire of classic recipes.

Teriyaki Casserole

Not every slow cooker recipe has to take all day. Try this one when you want a deep-down flavor in just 2 hours.

Cook on 190° for 3 hours,
or on 290° to 300° for 2 hours.
Makes 6 servings.

1 boneless sirloin or top round steak (about 1½ pounds)
3 tablespoons peanut oil or vegetable oil
1 clove garlic, halved
1 large onion, sliced and separated into rings
1 large green pepper, halved, seeded and sliced
1 large red pepper, halved, seeded and sliced
1 large zucchini, tipped and sliced
1 large yellow squash, tipped and sliced
½ pound mushrooms, sliced
1 large carrot, pared and cut into thin sticks
½ cup soy sauce
¼ cup saki or dry sherry
1 package (1 pound) Chinese noodles, cooked and drained
OR: 1 package (1 pound) fine noodles, cooked and drained

1 Cut very cold steak into very thin slices with a sharp knife.
2 Heat oil with garlic until very hot in a large skillet or slow cooker with a browning unit; remove garlic; brown beef quickly, a few pieces at a time; remove.
3 Add onion rings; sauté 2 minutes; add pepper slices, zucchini, yellow squash, mushrooms and carrots; sauté, stirring constantly, until vegetables glisten and have bright color; add soy sauce and saki or sherry. Spoon into slow cooker with steak.
4 Cook on low (190° to 200°) 3 hours, or on high (290° to 300°) 2 hours. Stir in noodles and spoon onto serving platter.

Dutch Spareribs

Country-style spareribs are simmered with sauerkraut and topped with caraway flavored dumplings

Cook on 190° to 200° for 8 hours.
Makes 6 servings.

3 pounds country-style spareribs, cut up
1 can (1 pound, 13 ounces) sauerkraut
2 tart apples, cored and cut into wedges
1 large onion, chopped (1 cup)
2 teaspoons seasoned salt
½ teaspoon seasoned pepper
¼ teaspoon caraway seeds, crushed
Dumplings (recipe follows)
2 cups sifted all-purpose flour
2 teaspoons baking powder
1 teaspoon salt
½ teaspoon caraway seeds
1 egg
¾ cup milk

1 Trim excess fat from spareribs; place in an electric slow cooker. Wash sauerkraut under running water; drain very well; place over ribs with apple wedges and onion; sprinkle with seasoned salt, seasoned pepper and caraway seeds; cover.
2 Cook on low (190° to 200°) 8 hours, or until ribs are very tender when pierced with a two-tined fork.

DUMPLINGS: Turn heat control to high (290° to 300°). Sift flour, baking powder and salt into a large bowl; stir in caraway seeds. Beat egg in a cup with a fork; beat in milk; pour, all at once, into dry mixture. Stir until blended. Uncover slow cooker. (If there is a level of liquid above the sauerkraut; remove some of the liquid with a bulb baster.) Drop dumplings by spoonfuls on top of sauerkraut; cover. Cook 30 minutes, or until dumplings are fluffy.

Polish Hot Pot

Red cabbage and pie-sliced apples turn this dish into a colorful, as well as flavorful family dish

Cook on 190° to 200° for 6 hours,
or on 290° to 300° for 3 hours.
Makes 4 servings.

1 keilbasa or Polish sausage (about 1 pound)
1 Bermuda onion, sliced
4 cups shredded red cabbage
1 can (1 pound, 4 ounces) pie-sliced apples
1 teaspoon salt
¼ teaspoon pepper
¼ teaspoon caraway seeds (optional)
1 bay leaf
½ cup beer
1 can condensed chicken broth

1 Score kielbasa all around and place in an electric slow cooker.
2 Layer onion, cabbage, and apples in cooker, sprinkling each with part of the salt and pepper; sprinkle with caraway, if used; add bay leaf. Pour beer and chicken broth over; cover cooker.
3 Cook on low (190° to 200°) for 6 hours, or on high (290° to 300°) 3 hours, or until cabbage is very tender. Spoon vegetables into a heated casserole; top with whole cooked sausage.

Cannellini Alla Catania

This Sicilian-style main dish feeds big appetites on a small budget

Cook on 190° to 200° for 10 hours,
or on 290° to 300° for 5 hours.
Makes 6 servings.

1 package (1 pound) dried cannellini beans (white kidney beans) or dried Great Northern beans
6 cups water
2 hot Italian sausages, sliced
1 large onion, chopped (1 cup)
1 large clove garlic, crushed
2 large ripe tomatoes, peeled and coarsely chopped
1 bay leaf, crumbled
½ teaspoon leaf thyme, crumbled
½ teaspoon leaf basil, crumbled
3 one-inch strips orange rind
1 teaspoon salt
¼ teaspoon pepper
1 envelope or teaspoon instant beef broth

1 Pick over beans and rinse. Cover beans with water in a large kettle; bring to boiling; cover; cook 2 minutes; remove from heat; let stand 1 hour. Pour into an electric slow cooker. (Or cover beans with water in slow cooker and soak overnight at room temperature.)
2 Brown sausages in a small skillet; push to one side; sauté onion and garlic in same pan until soft; stir in tomato, bay leaf, thyme, basil, orange strips, salt, pepper and instant beef broth; bring to boiling; stir into beans; cover.
3 Cook on low (190° to 200°) for 10 hours, or on high (290° to 300°) 5 hours, or until beans are tender. For a classic Italian dessert, serve an assortment of fruits and cheeses.
Suggested Variations: Dried lima beans can be substituted for the cannellini beans. Sweet Italian sausage, ¼ pound salami or 1 cup sliced pepperoni can be used instead of the hot Italian sausages.

French Pot Roast

Flavorful beef simmers fork-tender in canned onion soup

Cook on 190° to 200° for 10 hours,
or on 290° to 300° for 5 hours.
Makes 8 servings.

1 boneless round or chuck roast (about 4 pounds)
2 tablespoons all-purpose flour
2 tablespoons vegetable oil
1 can (10½ ounces) condensed onion soup
1 green pepper, seeded and cut into rings
¼ cup all-purpose flour
½ cup water

1 Trim excess fat from roast; rub beef well with flour; brown in oil in a large skillet or an electric slow cooker with a browning unit.
2 Place meat in slow cooker; pour onion soup over; cover cooker.
3 Cook on low (190° to 200°) 10 hours, or on high (290° to 300°) 5 hours, or until meat is tender when pierced with a two-tined fork. Place green pepper rings on roast to steam during last 10 minutes of cooking. Remove meat and pepper rings to heated serving platter; keep hot while making gravy.

4 Turn heat control to high (290° to 300°). Combine ¼ cup all-purpose flour and ½ cup cold water in a cup to make a smooth paste. Stir into slow cooker; cover; cook 15 minutes; taste and season with salt and pepper, if you wish.

Zurich Pork

A German influence is often noted in the cooking of this Swiss city

Cook on 190° to 200° for 10 hours,
or on 290° to 300° for 5 hours.
Makes 8 servings.

1 fresh pork shoulder butt (about 4 pounds)
2 teaspoons salt
1 teaspoon caraway seeds
¼ teaspoon pepper
2 large onions, peeled and cut into thick slices
1 large clove garlic, peeled
½ cup beer or water

1 Trim excess fat from pork; brown pork slowly in remaining fat in a heavy skillet or an electric slow cooker with a browning unit; drain off all fat.
2 Place meat in slow cooker. Sprinkle salt, caraway seeds and pepper over; add onions, garlic and beer or water; cover.
3 Cook on low (190° to 200°) 10 hours, or on high (290° to 300°) 5 hours, or until pork is tender when pierced with a fork.
4 Remove to carving board or heated serving platter; discard garlic. Spoon onions around meat. Serve with refrigerated crescent rolls.

Irish Lamb Stew

Traditionally, the lamb is not browned in making Irish stew. Peas add color and flavor when cooked just before serving

Cook on 190° to 200° for 8 hours,
or on 290° to 300° for 4 hours.
Makes 6 servings.

2 pounds lean boneless lamb shoulder, cubed
18 small white onions, peeled
1 pound carrots, pared and cut into 1-inch pieces
2 teaspoons salt
¼ teaspoon pepper
2 envelopes or teaspoons instant chicken broth
1 teaspoon leaf basil, crumbled
½ teaspoon leaf thyme, crumbled
1 clove garlic, minced
2 cups water
1 package (10 ounces) frozen green peas, thawed
1 cup shredded lettuce

1 Layer lamb, onions and carrots in an electric slow cooker; season with salt, pepper, instant chicken broth, basil, thyme and garlic; pour water over; cover slow cooker.
2 Cook on low (190° to 200°) 8 hours, or on high (290° to 300°) 4 hours, or until lamb is tender.
3 Turn heat control to high (290° to 300°). Add peas and lettuce; stir to blend well; cover. Simmer 30 minutes. Serve with slices of brown soda bread.

ELECTRIC SLOW COOKER SAFETY

The gift that allows you to relax at work while dinner is cooking can only do its job if you know how it can help you and how it cannot.

Before you cook: *However glamorous your slow cooker is, it is put together by machines—and its efficiency is not always consistent with the manufacturer's leaflet. So, before you fill it with goodness, pour in cold tap water to the half-full mark. Cover and turn the high-heating setting on. If the water boils before 2½ hours, reduce the cooking time of the recipes in this book. But, if more than 3 hours goes by before boiling, add to the cooking time.*

Bacteria hurts: *Most foods if left unattended for more than four hours will develop bacteria (or food spoilage) on the top. Since your crockery cooker cooks slowly, there is a chance of food spoilage if you attempt to cook meats or eggs at a low temperature for less than six hours. To be on the safe side, faithfully follow the recipe directions.*

Also, don't be misled into believing that your make-ahead foods can be stored in your cooker overnight. Place all made-ahead foods in the refrigerator and transfer to the cooker when you start the cooker doing its job.

And, as soon as the cooker is through, remove the food from the cooker and store in the refrigerator.

Aldilla

Try this south-of-the-border steak dish with chili powder and hot chili pepper for a dish with a dash

Cook on 190° to 200° for 8 hours,
or on 290° to 300° for 4 hours.
Makes 6 servings.

1 flank steak (about 1½ pounds)
2 to 4 teaspoons chili powder
½ cup all-purpose flour
1½ teaspoons salt
½ teaspoon seasoned pepper
3 tablespoons vegetable oil
1 large onion, chopped (1 cup)
1 large carrot, pared and chopped
1 large green pepper, halved, seeded and chopped
2 large ripe tomatoes, peeled and chopped
¼ cup dry red wine
1 hot chili pepper, seeded (from a 4-ounce can)

1 Score steak and rub with chili powder; coat with a mixture of flour, ½ teaspoon salt and ¼ teaspoon of the seasoned pepper; pound steak on both sides with a wooden mallet or the edge of a plate to tenderize; cut into 6 pieces.
2 Brown steak in hot oil in a large skillet or an electric slow cooker with a browning unit; remove and reserve. Sauté onion, carrot, green pepper and tomato in pan drippings; add remaining 1 teaspoon salt and ¼ teaspoon seasoned pepper; remove from heat.
3 Combine steak and sautéed vegetables in slow cooker; add wine and hot chili pepper; cover.
4 Cook on low (190° to 200°) 8 hours, or on high (290° to 300°) 4 hours, or until meat is tender. Serve with cornbread and an avocado, ripe olive and shredded lettuce salad, if you wish.

Koenigsberger Klops

A classic German meat ball dish garnished with lemon slices and capers

Cook on 190° to 200° for 5 hours.
Makes 6 servings.

1 pound ground beef
1 pound ground pork
1 medium-size onion, chopped (½ cup)
½ cup packaged dry bread crumbs
1½ teaspoons salt
¼ teaspoon pepper
Dash ground nutmeg
4 eggs
1 can (10½ ounces) condensed beef broth
1 cup water
1 large onion, peeled and quartered
¼ cup cider vinegar
1 tablespoon sugar
1 teaspoon mixed pickling spices

1 Combine ground beef and pork, chopped onion, crumbs, 1 teaspoon of the salt, pepper and nutmeg in a medium-size bowl until well-blended.
2 Separate eggs, putting whites into a large bowl and yolks into a small bowl; cover and refrigerate. Beat whites until they form soft peaks; fold into meat mixture. Shape into 1-inch balls and place in an electric slow cooker.
3 Combine beef broth, water, onion, vinegar, sugar, mixed pickling spices and remaining ½ teaspoon salt in a small saucepan. Bring to boiling; lower heat and simmer 15 minutes; strain into slow cooker; cover.
4 Cook on low (190° to 200°) 5 hours; remove meat balls to a heated deep serving platter and keep warm.
5 Turn heat control to high (290° to 300°). Combine 1 tablespoon all-purpose flour with 2 tablespoons cold water in a cup; stir into liquid in cooker until smooth; cover. Cook 15 minutes; beat saved egg yolks with a fork; beat in 1 cup of hot sauce; return to cooker; cook 5 minutes; then pour over meat balls. Garnish with lemon slices and capers; serve with boiled parslied potatoes and mugs of dark ale, if you wish.

English Hot Pot

British cooks have made these one pot specialties for generations

Cook on 190° to 200° for 8 hours,
or on 290° to 300° for 4 hours.
Makes 8 servings.

2 pounds boneless lamb shoulder, cubed
¼ cup all-purpose flour
2 envelopes or teaspoons instant chicken broth
2 teaspoons salt
1 teaspoon leaf oregano, crumbled
½ teaspoon leaf rosemary, crumbled
¼ teaspoon pepper
1 large onion, sliced and separated into rings

For those who love sweet-sour taste of sauerkraut and sausages try **Munich Kraut** and Knockwurst.

3 small yellow squash, cut into 2-inch pieces
12 small potatoes, pared and halved
1 cup boiling water
2 tablespoons butter or margarine, melted

1 Trim all excess fat from lamb. Shake cubes, part at a time, in flour in a plastic bag to coat well.
2 Mix instant chicken broth, salt, oregano, rosemary and pepper in a cup.
3 Layer meat and vegetables into an electric slow cooker this way: Half of each of the lamb, onion and squash, sprinkling each layer with seasoning mixture. Repeat with remaining lamb, vegetables and seasoning mixture.
4 Lay potatoes, rounded side up, on top; pour boiling water over. Brush potatoes with butter; cover.
5 Cook on low (190° to 200°) 8 hours, or on high (290° to 300°) 4 hours, or until meat and vegetables are tender. Serve with hearts of lettuce and cold apple cider, if you wish.

Munich Kraut and Knockwurst

Try this slow-cooker version of Choucroute a l'Alsacienne

Cook on 190° to 200° for 6 hours,
or on 290° to 300° for 3 hours.
Makes 4 servings.

1 large onion, sliced
¼ cup (½ stick) butter or margarine
1 large red apple, quartered, cored and diced
1 can (1 pound, 13 ounces) sauerkraut, washed and drained
3 tablespoons brown sugar
1 teaspoon caraway seeds
1 pound knockwursts, scored
½ cup beer or dry white wine

1 Sauté onion in 3 tablespoons butter or margarine in a large skillet or slow cooker with a

(continued)

browning unit just until soft; sauté apple 2 minutes. Stir in sauerkraut, brown sugar and caraway seeds; toss lightly with a fork to mix well.
2 Sauté knockwursts in remaining 1 tablespoon butter or margarine in same pan 5 minutes, or until browned; arrange on sauerkraut in slow cooker; drizzle beer or wine over; cover slow cooker.
3 Cook on low (190° to 200°) 6 hours or on high (290° to 300°) 3 hours. Spoon sauerkraut into heated casserole and top with knockwurst. Serve with a zippy mustard, dill pickles and pumpernickel bread, if you wish.

Dutch Hot Pot

Coriander seeds and leaf thyme add the distinctive touch to this Amsterdam dish

Cook on 190° to 200° for 8 hours,
or on 290° to 300° for 4 hours.
Makes 8 servings.

2 pounds boneless pork shoulder, cubed
¼ cup all-purpose flour
1 tablespoon salt
1 teaspoon leaf thyme, crumbled
1 teaspoon coriander seeds, crushed
¼ teaspoon pepper
1 can (1 pound) red kidney beans
boiling water
4 medium-size potatoes, pared and cut into ¼-inch thick slices
4 medium-size onions, sliced and separated into rings
8 carrots, pared and cut in 4-inch lengths
2 tablespoons butter or margarine

1 Trim excess fat from pork. Shake cubes, part at a time, with flour in a plastic bag to coat well.
2 Mix salt, thyme, coriander seeds and pepper in a cup; reserve.
3 Drain liquid from kidney beans into a 2-cup measure; add boiling water to make 1½ cups.
4 Layer vegetables and meat into an electric slow cooker this way: Half each of potatoes, onions, pork, kidney beans and carrots, sprinkling each layer lightly with seasoning mixture. Repeat with remaining vegetables, pork and seasoning mixture for a second layer.
5 Pour liquid over; dot with butter or margarine; cover.
6 Cook on low (190° to 200°) 8 hours, or on high (290° to 300°) 4 hours, or until meat and vegetables are tender. Serve with dark beer, if you wish.

Bermuda Lamb Stew

A delightfully mild-seasoned dish with a springtime flavor

Cook on 190° to 200° for 8 hours,
or on 290° to 300° for 4 hours.
Makes 6 servings.

2 pounds boneless lamb shoulder, cubed
1 Bermuda onion, thinly sliced and separated into rings
2 cups shredded lettuce
2 medium-size ripe tomatoes, chopped
2 pounds fresh peas, shelled (2 cups)
OR: 2 cups frozen peas (from a 1½-pound bag), thawed
2 medium-size yellow squash, cut into 2-inch pieces
2 teaspoons salt
½ teaspoon leaf rosemary, crumbled
¼ teaspoon freshly ground pepper
1 envelope or teaspoon instant chicken broth
1 cup hot water
3 tablespoons cornstarch

1 Trim all excess fat from lamb. Place lamb in the bottom of an electric slow cooker; add onion rings, lettuce, tomatoes, peas, squash, salt, rosemary and pepper to cover lamb.
2 Dissolve instant broth in hot water in a 2-cup measure; pour over meat and vegetables; stir to mix well; cover.
3 Cook on low (190° to 200°) 8 hours, or on high (290° to 300°) 4 hours, or until lamb is tender.
4 Turn heat control to high (290° to 300°). Combine cornstarch and ⅓ cup cold water in a cup; stir into liquid until well-blended. Cover; simmer 15 minutes longer, until bubbly-hot.

Australian Lamb "Roasts"

Lamb shanks are a meaty treat. Look for them on special, especially in the spring

Cook on 190° to 200° for 8 hours,
or on 290° to 300° for 4 hours.
Makes 4 servings.

4 lamb shanks (about 3 pounds)
1 large onion, chopped (1 cup)

1 clove garlic, minced
1 cup dry white wine
2 teaspoons salt
½ teaspoon pepper
1 bay leaf
2 tablespoons all-purpose flour
¼ cup water

1 Trim excess fat from lamb shanks. Brown lamb in its remaining fat in a large skillet or an electric slow cooker with a browning unit; remove and reserve.
2 Add onion and garlic to pan; sauté just until soft. Stir in wine, salt, pepper and bay leaf; remove from heat.
3 Combine lamb shanks and wine mixture in slow cooker; cover.
4 Cook on low (190° to 200°) 8 hours, or on high (290° to 300°) 4 hours, or until lamb shanks are tender. Remove to a heated serving platter and keep warm.
5 Turn heat control to high (290° to 300°). Combine flour and water in a cup. Stir into liquid in slow cooker; cover. Cook 15 minutes. Pass in gravy boat.

Beef Burgundy

This recipe takes a little time, but the resulting dish will make your reputation as a cook

Cook on 190° to 200° for 8 hours,
or on 290° to 300° for 4 hours.
Makes 8 servings.

½ pound thickly sliced bacon
2 pounds lean boneless beef chuck, cubed
1 large onion, chopped (1 cup)
1 cup finely chopped carrot
1 cup finely chopped celery
2 cloves garlic, minced
2 teaspoons salt
1 teaspoon leaf thyme, crumbled
1 bay leaf
¼ teaspoon pepper
2 cups dry red wine
¼ cup all-purpose flour
1 pound mushrooms
1 bunch leeks
1 bunch carrots
¼ cup (½ stick) butter or margarine
1 envelope or teaspoon instant chicken broth
½ cup water

1 Cut bacon into 1-inch pieces; place in a saucepan; cover with water. Bring to boiling; lower heat and simmer 10 minutes. Dry bacon on paper towels. Fry bacon until crisp in a large skillet or an electric slow cooker with a browning unit. Remove bacon and reserve; pour off all but 2 tablespoons of the bacon fat into a cup.
2 Brown beef, a few pieces at a time, in fat; remove and reserve; Sauté onion, carrot, celery and garlic in pan drippings, adding more bacon fat, if needed; stir in salt, thyme, bay leaf and pepper.
3 Place beef in cooker with vegetable mixture; add wine; cover cooker.
4 Cook on low (190° to 200°) 8 hours, or on high (290° to 300°) 4 hours; remove bay leaf. Remove beef from liquid with slotted spoon; keep warm in a heated casserole.
5 Pour liquid, half at a time, into an electric blender container; add flour, half at a time; cover container; whirl at high speed 1 minute. (Or press liquid through a sieve with a wooden spoon into a bowl; cool slightly; stir in flour until well-blended.) Pour liquid into a large saucepan; bring to boiling. Cook, stirring constantly, until sauce thickens and bubbles 3 minutes longer.
6 One hour before serving, wipe mushrooms with damp paper towel; flute mushrooms by marking the center of each cap with a small, sharp paring knife. Starting there, make a curved cut, about ⅛-inch deep, to edge. Repeat around to make 8 even cuts. Now make a second cut just behind each line, angling knife so you can lift out a narrow strip; set mushrooms aside. Cut leeks into 5-inch pieces and halve; wash well to remove all sand; pare and cut carrots into 5-inch pieces.
7 Sauté mushrooms in butter or margarine in a large skillet; remove; sauté leeks lightly in skillet; remove; add carrots and sauté 5 minutes; add instant chicken broth and water to skillet; cover and simmer 15 minutes, or until carrots are almost tender; push to one side. Return mushrooms and leeks to skillet. Cover; simmer 10 minutes, or until vegetables are tender.
8 Surround beef with vegetables; sprinkle beef with cooked bacon. Pour vegetable liquid in skillet into sauce, pour over beef and vegetables.

HOSTESS TIP: The finished dish can be held in a very slow oven (275°) for 1 hour before serving. Beef can be cooked and sauce made the day before. Cool, then cover and refrigerate. One hour before serving, place casserole in oven. Set oven control on moderate (350°) and bake 1 hour, or until bubbly-hot, while preparing vegetables.

KNOW YOUR CROCKERY COOKER

They may all look alike, but there are basic differences among crockery cookers—they have a heating element in the bottom, sit on a separate heating unit, or have heating wires wrapped around the sides of the cookers.

Heating element in the bottom: *As the heating unit turns on and off, regulated by the thermostat, it's best to use this type of cooker only when you are able to give an occasional stir. Otherwise the food on the bottom of the cooker may stick.*

Heating unit on the bottom: *Similar to the one above, again you should not use this type of cooker if the recipe is an all-day one and you will not be home to make that occasional stir. But when you can baby-sit your crocker, this type of unit works well.*

Heating element around the sides: *This type of cooker works best for at-home or away-from-home cooking. Because the heat is constant, top to bottom of the cooker, there is no gradual heating up from the bottom. Also, in recipes which call for long cooking, there is no chance of food spoilage at the top of the cooker.*

Brazilian Feijoada

Black bean soup is a favorite in all Latin American countries. This is the slow-cooker method of preparing it

Cook on 190° to 200° for 8 hours,
or on 290° to 300° for 4 hours.
Makes 12 servings.

2 bags (1 pound each) dried black beans
10 cups water
1 boneless smoked pork butt (about 2 pounds)
½ pound pepperoni, cut into ½-inch pieces
3 large onions, sliced
2 cups dry red wine or beef broth
2 teaspoons salt
3 oranges, peeled and sectioned
¼ cup chopped parsley

1 Pick over beans and rinse under running water. Combine beans with water in a large kettle or a 5-quart electric slow cooker; bring to boiling and boil 2 minutes; cover. Remove from heat; let stand 1 hour; add pork butt, pepperoni, onions, wine or beef broth and salt; cover.
2 Cook on low (190° to 200°) 8 hours, stirring after 4 hours, if possible, or on high (290° to 300°) 4 hours, stirring after 2 hours, if possible, or until beans and meat are tender.
3 Remove pork butt; press beans against the side of the slow cooker with a wooden spoon to mash some of them. Serve with orange sections and chopped parsley arranged atop beans.
4 Slice pork butt thinly and pass it around, on a separate plate, with mustard and whole-wheat bread.

Persian Steak Roll

Wheat pilaf and spinach are the special ingredients that makes this recipe out of the ordinary

Cook on 190° to 200° for 10 hours,
or on 290° to 300° for 5 hours.
Makes 6 servings.

1 flank steak (about 1½ pounds)
1 small onion, chopped (¼ cup)
4 tablespoons vegetable oil
½ cup wheat pilaf (from a 12-ounce package)
1 teaspoon curry powder
1 cup water
1 package (10 ounces) frozen chopped spinach, thawed
1 can (1 pound) red kidney beans
½ teaspoon cardamom seeds, crushed
1½ teaspoons salt
¼ teaspoon pepper
1 can (1 pound) stewed tomatoes
1 tablespoon lemon juice

1 Ask your meatman to split flank steak, butterfly fashion. Or, at home, split it yourself, working slowly with a sharp long-blade knife and cutting with a sawing motion as evenly as possible. Pound steak with a mallet or rolling pin to make it evenly thin.
2 Sauté onion in 2 tablespoons of the oil until soft in a large skillet. Stir in wheat pilaf; cook 2 minutes, or until lightly browned. Stir in curry powder and water; cover skillet.
3 Bring to boiling, then simmer 15 minutes, or until liquid is absorbed. Cool slightly; spread over meat in a thin layer.
4 Drain spinach, then pat as dry as possible between paper towels.
5 Drain kidney beans, saving liquid. Mix beans, spinach, cardamom seeds and ½ tea-

spoon of the salt in a medium-size bowl; spread over pilaf layer.

6 Starting at one long side, roll up tightly, tucking in any loose stuffing; tie with string every 2 inches. Sprinkle with remaining 1 teaspoon salt and pepper.

7 Brown roll in remaining 2 tablespoons oil in the large skillet or in an electric slow cooker with a browning unit; remove and reserve.

8 Stir tomatoes, lemon juice and saved bean liquid into pan until well-blended.

9 Place the stuffed meat roll and sauce in slow cooker; cover.

10 Cook on low (190° to 200°) 10 hours, turning meat after 5 hours, if possible, or on high (290° to 300°) 5 hours, turning meat after 3 hours, if possible. Place meat on heated serving platter and remove strings. Cut into 1-inch slices and serve with pan sauce.

Swiss Cabbage Rolls

Try serving these delicious rolls with a dollop of sour cream on top

Cook on 190° to 200° for 8 hours,
or on 290° to 300° for 4 hours.
Makes 6 servings.

12 large cabbage leaves
1 pound ground meatloaf mixture
2 cups cooked rice
1 small onion, chopped (¼ cup)
1 egg
1 teaspoon salt
¼ teaspoon pepper
Dash ground nutmeg
¼ cup all-purpose flour
2 tablespoons vegetable shortening
1 can (10¾ ounces) condensed tomato soup
1 teaspoon cider vinegar
1 teaspoon Worcestershire sauce

1 Trim base of cabbage and carefully break off 12 whole leaves. (Save remaining cabbage for another day.)

2 Place leaves in a large saucepan; pour in boiling water and cover; let stand 5 minutes; drain on paper towels; trim off the coarse rib on the back of each leaf with a sharp paring knife.

3 Combine meatloaf mixture, rice, onion, egg, salt, pepper and nutmeg in a medium-size bowl; mix.

4 Lay cabbage leaves flat on a wooden board; spoon meat mixture into the middle of each, dividing evenly. Fold edges of each leaf over filling and roll up; fasten with wooden picks.

5 Coat cabbage rolls with flour on wax paper. Sauté rolls, a few at a time, in shortening in a large skillet or an electric slow cooker with a browning unit.

6 Place cabbage rolls in slow cooker; pour tomato soup, vinegar and Worcestershire sauce over; cover.

7 Cook on low (190° to 200°) 8 hours, or on high (290° to 300°) 4 hours. Serve with a topping of dairy sour cream.

Suggested Variations: Cooked brown rice or kasha can be substituted for the cooked rice. Ground beef or pork can be used in place of the meatloaf mixture.

Hungarian Lamb

Eggplant and sour cream give the distinctive flavors to this dish

Cook on 190° to 200° for 8 hours,
or on 290° to 300° for 4 hours.
Makes 6 servings.

1½ pounds lean lamb shoulder, cubed
¼ cup all-purpose flour
1 teaspoon salt
¼ teaspoon pepper
3 tablespoons vegetable oil
2 envelopes instant beef broth
1½ cups water
12 small white onions, peeled
1 small eggplant, pared and diced
1 cup dairy sour cream
1 teaspoon paprika

1 Shake lamb with flour, salt and pepper in a plastic bag to coat well.

2 Brown quickly in oil in an electric slow cooker with a browning unit, or a large skillet; stir in instant beef broth and water; bring to boiling.

3 Combine lamb mixture, onions and eggplant in slow cooker; cover.

4 Cook on low (190° to 200°) 8 hours, or on high (290° to 300°) 4 hours, or until lamb and onions are tender.

5 Stir 1 cup of hot mixture into sour cream and paprika in a medium-size bowl; return to cooker and stir to blend.

A one-dish meal that will spin your head, **Dutch Hot Pot** teams with red kidney beans, potatoes, carrots, thyme, and coriander. (See page 86.)

Oxtails Romano

This recipe was inspired by a Roman trattoria specialty; Serve with linguini

Cook on 290° to 300° for 2 hours,
then on 190° to 200° for 8 hours.
Makes 6 servings.

3 pounds oxtails, cut up
3 tablespoons olive oil or vegetable oil
1 large onion, chopped (1 cup)
2 cups chopped celery
2 cloves garlic, minced
2 large carrots, pared and diced
⅓ cup chopped parsley
1 can (1 pound, 1 ounce) Italian tomatoes
1 cup beef broth
2 teaspoons salt
½ teaspoon freshly ground pepper

1 Brown oxtails, a few pieces at a time, in oil in an electric slow cooker with a browning unit or a large skillet; remove and keep warm. Sauté onion, celery, garlic, carrots and parsley in drippings until soft.

2 Stir in tomatoes, beef broth, salt and pepper until sauce bubbles. Combine oxtails and vegetables in slow cooker; cover.

3 Cook on high (290° to 300°) 2 hours. Turn heat control to low (190° to 200°) and cook for 8 hours, or until oxtails are so tender that meat falls from bones.

4 Unplug slow cooker and let mixture cool five minutes for fat to rise to the surface; skim off fat. Serve with buttered linguini and a tossed green salad.

Black Forest Beef Platter

Pot roasts are more flavorful and tender when treated to slow, gentle cooking

Cook on 190° to 200° for 10 hours,
or on 290° to 300° for 5 hours.
Makes 8 servings.

1 boneless chuck roast (about 4 pounds)
1 cup water
¼ cup chili sauce

1 envelope (2 to a package) onion soup mix
1 tablespoon caraway seeds, crushed
1 tablespoon paprika
¼ teaspoon pepper
1 can (1 pound, 11 ounces) sauerkraut, drained
¼ cup firmly packed brown sugar
1 container (8 ounces) dairy sour cream

1 Trim excess fat from roast; brown in its remaining fat in a large skillet or an electric slow cooker with a browning unit; remove and reserve.
2 Stir in water, chili sauce, onion soup mix, caraway seeds, paprika and pepper; bring to boiling.
3 Place meat with sauce in slow cooker; mix sauerkraut and brown sugar in a medium-size bowl; stir into liquid around meat; cover.
4 Cook on low (190° to 200°) 10 hours, or on high (290° to 300°) 5 hours, or until meat is very tender. Remove to a carving board; keep hot while finishing sauce for the sauerkraut.
5 Stir about ½ cup of the hot sauerkraut mixture into sour cream in a medium-size bowl; then stir back into remaining sauerkraut mixture in slow cooker. Heat just until hot, about 5 minutes.
6 Spoon sauerkraut into a deep serving platter. Carve meat into ¼-inch thick slices; place on top of sauerkraut. Serve with buttered noodles, if you wish.

Picadillo

This Cuban supper dish is usually served with rice and fried bananas

Cook on 190° to 200° for 6 hours.
Makes 8 servings.

1 large onion, chopped (1 cup)
1 large green pepper, halved, seeded and chopped
1 clove garlic, minced
¼ cup olive oil
4 large ripe tomatoes, peeled and chopped
½ teaspoon sugar
3 cups finely diced cooked beef
1 can (10½ ounces) condensed beef broth
1 teaspoon salt
1 bay leaf
¼ teaspoon ground cloves

1 Sauté onion, green pepper and garlic in oil in a large skillet or an electric slow cooker with a browning unit until soft; stir in tomatoes and sugar; simmer 5 minutes. Stir in diced beef.
2 Combine in slow cooker with beef broth, salt, bay leaf and cloves; cover.
3 Cook on low (190° to 200°) 6 hours, or until ready to serve.

Cocido

Frugal Iberian cooks combine sausage with beef, chick peas and cabbage to satisfy appetites and save pesetas, all at the same time

Cook on 190° to 200° for 10 hours,
or on 290° to 300° for 5 hours.
Makes 6 servings.

2 pounds lean chuck, cut into 1-inch cubes
1 tablespoon salt
2 cloves garlic, chopped
4 cups water
1 bay leaf coarsely crumbled
6 peppercorns
6 whole coriander seeds
1 large onion, sliced
4 carrots, pared and cut into 1-inch pieces
4 potatoes, pared and cut into 1-inch cubes
2 cans (1 pound, 4 ounces each) chick-peas, drained
3 tablespoons chopped parsley
3 cups shredded cabbage
1 large leek, washed and cut into ¼-inch slices (about 1 cup)
6 pork sausages (½ pound)

1 Combine beef, salt, garlic and water in a slow cooker. Tie bay leaf, peppercorns and coriander seeds in cheesecloth; add to cooker with onion, carrots, potatoes, chick-peas and 2 tablespoons of the parsley.
2 Cook on low (190° to 200°) 10 hours or high (290° to 300°) 5 hours. Stir in cabbage and leek. Cook 20 minutes longer. Remove cheesecloth bag. Thicken, if desired, with a little flour mixed with water.
3 About 15 minutes before serving, brown sausages in a skillet, 10 to 15 minutes; cut them in half and arrange on top of stew. Sprinkle with remaining parsley.
4 Serve in soup plates or shallow bowls with crusty bread, if you wish.

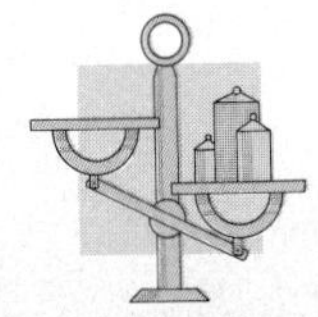

County Kerry Pork Roast

Fresh pork shoulder makes an especially delicious gravy to spoon over fluffy, buttered mashed potatoes

Cook on 190° to 200° for 10 hours,
or on 290° to 300° for 5 hours.
Makes 8 servings.

1 fresh picnic or shoulder butt (about 5 pounds)
1 large onion, chopped (1 cup)
1 teaspoon leaf marjoram, crumbled
¾ cup bottled barbecue sauce
¾ cup water

1 Trim excess fat from pork; place in an electric slow cooker; sprinkle with onion and marjoram; pour mixture of barbecue sauce and water over; cover.
2 Cook on low (190° to 200°) 10 hours, or on high (290° to 300°) 5 hours, or until pork is tender when pierced with a fork.
3 Slice hot and serve with mashed potatoes, steamed cabbage and horseradish mustard, if you wish.

Suggested Variations: Fresh ham, pork loin or lamb shoulder can be substituted for the pork shoulder in this recipe. Also, use leaf savory instead of marjoram.

Ensenada Chili Pot

There's South-of-the-border flavor in this no-watch special

Cook on 190° to 200° for 8 hours,
or on 290° to 300° for 4 hours.
Makes 8 servings.

2 pounds lean boneless chuck, cubed
¼ cup all-purpose flour
1 to 2 tablespoons chili powder
2 teaspoons salt
¼ teaspoon pepper
¼ cup vegetable shortening
1 large onion, chopped (1 cup)
2 cans (1 pound each) red kidney beans
1 can (1 pound, 13 ounces) tomatoes
1 can (12 or 16 ounces) whole-kernel corn
1 can (4 ounces) pimiento, sliced
1 can (4 ounces) green chili peppers, seeded and chopped
Hot cooked rice
Shredded Cheddar cheese

1 Trim excess fat from beef; shake beef cubes with flour, chili powder, salt and pepper in a plastic bag to coat well.
2 Brown, a few at a time, in shortening in a large skillet or an electric slow cooker with a browning unit; remove and reserve. Stir in onion; sauté 5 minutes, or until onion is soft. Spoon off any excess drippings; stir any remaining flour-seasoning mixture into pan.
3 Drain liquid from kidney beans and add to pan; stir in tomatoes; bring to boiling; remove from heat.
4 Place beef in slow cooker with tomato mixture; stir in kidney beans and corn; cover cooker.
5 Cook on low (190° to 200°) 8 hours, or on high (290° to 300°) 4 hours; stir in pimiento and green chili peppers.
6 Spoon chili over rice in soup bowls. Top with shredded Cheddar cheese.

Lamb Chops Polynesian

Thrifty pork shoulder chops can also be used in this recipe

Cook on 190° to 200° for 8 hours,
or on 290° to 300° for 4 hours.
Makes 6 servings.

6 shoulder lamb chops, cut ¾-inch thick
2 teaspoons curry powder
2 tablespoons vegetable oil
1 large onion, chopped (1 cup)
1 clove garlic, minced
1½ teaspoons salt
1 teaspoon ground allspice
1 cup water
¼ cup lemon juice
1 jar (about 8 ounces) junior prunes (baby-pack)
1 jar (about 8 ounces) junior applesauce-and-apricots (baby-pack)

1 Trim excess fat from chops. Rub lamb with curry powder. Brown slowly in oil in a large skillet or slow cooker with a browning unit; remove.
2 Sauté onion and garlic until soft in same pan; stir in salt, allspice, water and lemon juice. Bring to boiling; stir in junior fruits.
3 Place lamb chops in slow cooker with fruit sauce; cover.
4 Cook on low (190° to 200°) 8 hours, or on high (290° to 300°) 4 hours, or until tender. Serve with fried rice and sautéed bananas, if you wish.

Seville Pot Roast

Colorful stuffed-olive rings dot each slice of this savory roast

Cook on 190° to 200° for 10 hours,
or on 290° to 300° for 6 hours.
Makes 8 servings.

1 round, rump or boneless chuck roast (about 4 pounds)
1 jar (about 5 ounces) stuffed green olives
1 medium-size onion, chopped (½ cup)
1 jar (about 5 ounces) junior strained carrots (baby-pack)
1 cup water
1 tablespoon instant coffee powder
1 tablespoon sugar
1 teaspoon salt
¼ teaspoon pepper
½ cup light cream
2 tablespoons all-purpose flour

1 Trim excess fat from beef; make slashes about 1½ inches deep and 2 inches apart all the way around meat with a sharp knife; push an olive deep into each cut.
2 Brown beef in a large skillet or an electric slow cooker with a browning unit; remove and reserve.
3 Sauté onion until soft in same pan; stir in carrots, water, instant coffee, sugar, salt and pepper. Place beef with onion mixture in slow cooker; cover.
4 Cook on low (190° to 200°) 10 hours, or on high (290° to 300°) 6 hours, or until beef is tender when pierced with a two-tined fork. Remove beef to serving platter and keep warm.
5 Turn heat control to high (290° to 300°). Combine cream and flour in a cup. Stir into liquid until well-blended; cover; simmer 15 minutes.
6 Carve meat into ¼-inch thick slices and pass gravy separately. Serve with saffron rice, if you wish.

HOSTESS TIP: To prepare saffron rice, crush about 3 strands of saffron and stir into cooking water for rice. For 8 servings of 1 cup each, you will need 2 cups uncooked rice.

There's more to **Pot Roast Seville** than meets the eye. Not shown here, each slice of beef is dotted with stuffed olives. You'll enjoy the flavor.

Hong Kong Pork Stew

If you like sweet-and-sour pork, you'll rave about this colorful stew

Cook on 190° to 200° for 8 hours,
or on 290° to 300° for 4 hours.
Makes 8 servings.

2 pounds boneless pork shoulder, cubed
1 teaspoon salt
¼ teaspoon ground ginger
⅛ teaspoon pepper
1 can (13¼ ounces) pineapple chunks
¼ cup firmly packed brown sugar
1 envelope or teaspoon instant chicken broth
¼ cup light molasses
¼ cup vinegar
2 tablespoons cornstarch
1 can (1 pound) sweet potatoes
2 firm tomatoes, cut in eighths
1 green pepper, halved, seeded and cut in 1-inch squares

1 Trim excess fat from pork; place in an electric slow cooker; season with salt, ginger and pepper.
2 Drain syrup from pineapple, adding water to syrup to make 1½ cups; reserve pineapple chunks. Add syrup mixture to pork; stir in sugar, instant broth, molasses and vinegar; cover.
3 Cook on low (190° to 200°) 8 hours, or on high (290° to 300°) 4 hours.
4 Turn heat control to high (290° to 300°). Combine cornstarch and ¼ cup cold water in a cup; stir into pork mixture until well-blended.
5 Add sweet potatoes, tomatoes, pineapple chunks and green pepper; cover; simmer 20 minutes longer.

INDEX

T-Z